BEYOND
5 STAR
FINANCE

Beyond 5-Star Finance: Taking Your Financial Window from Swollen Shut to Swung Open

Co-Authored by:
Joyce Addis
Chris Bowen

Cover design by: Joe DeLeon

ISBN: 978-1-950718-37-5   1 2 3 4 5 6 7 8 9 10

Printed in the United States of America

⋆ ⋆ ⋆ ⋆ ⋆

BEYOND 5 STAR FINANCE

[
**TAKING YOUR
FINANCIAL WINDOW
FROM SWOLLEN SHUT
TO SWUNG OPEN**
]

⋆ ⋆ ⋆ ⋆ ⋆

DR. CHRIS BOWEN

FOREWORD BY DR. SAM CHAND

**DREAM
RELEASER
ENTERPRISES**

CONTENTS

Foreword. vii

Part 1: 25 Things That Will Close
The Windows of Heaven. 9

Reason #1—Not Tithing 11

Reason #2—Wrong Priorities 17

Reason #3—Double-Mindedness 21

Reason #4—Unaccepted Offerings 23

Reason #5—Not Understanding 25

Reason #6—Fear. 31

Reason #7—No Faith. 35

Reason #8—Unbelief 37

Reason #9—Wrong Desires. 41

Reason #10—Looking Back. 43

Reason #11—Wrong Marital Relationships. 47

Reason #12—Discord With The Brethren 51

Reason #13—Not Trusting God's Man 55

Reason #14—Not Working 59

Reason #15—No Patience 63

Reason #16—Improper Thinking. 67

Reason #17—Improper Talking 69

Reason #18—Unpaid Vows. 73

Reason #19—Unjust Stewardship 77

Reason #20—Not Discerning The Body 81

Reason #21—Loving Money. 85

Reason #22—Improper Upbringing. 89

Reason #23—Not Hearing The Poor 93

Reason #24—Hidden Sin. 97

Reason #25—Tradition 103

Part 2: Ten Steps To Financial Freedom 105

Step #1—Accessing Your Ability To Get Wealth 107

Step #2—Accepting Your Responsibility of Tithing. . . .119

Step #3—Allowing The Great Physician
                To Do Plastic Surgery. .125

Step #4—Acquiring A Taste For Good Stewardship . . .131

Step #5—Admitting Your Need For A Budget 151

Step #6—Allotting Room For Monument Offerings . . .157

Step #7—Achieving The Principle of Sowing. 161

Step #8—Always Realizing the Power of Your Seed . . .173

Step #9—Allowing Your Harvest
                To Reap Your Benefits 181

Step #10—Always Expecting Your
                Manifested Abundance. 187

FOREWORD

BEYOND 5-STAR FINANCES IS A FRONTAL ATTACK on the enemy who does not want you to prosper. Have you noticed that the biggest area of God's desire to bless you is also the same area the enemy attacks? In fact, many don't need to be attacked anymore; they're already in bondage. The enemy knows that, as long as we do not walk into our blessing, we will not be able to be a blessing.

So many mouth the popular cliché, "I'm blessed to be a blessing." However, many of these same people can *truly* swing open what has been swollen shut and become the conduit of blessing they were always meant to be. In the Bible, Jesus spoke more about finances than the subjects of heaven and hell combined! He knew that the battle would be in the realm of understanding what this book is all about.

I have known Dr. Chris and Kathy Bowen since they were teen-agers. I had the privilege of marrying them. I have found Sister Joyce Addis, in the short time I have known her, as a wealth of knowledge in the arena of finances. I have seen the authors apply the biblical principles in this book and live lives of blessing and integrity. You can too!

There are some things I especially appreciate in their approach to this book:

- A balanced view of prosperity. It is more than money. Money is one slice of the pie—the others are spiritual prosperity, health, a happy marriage, a good church, a place of service, believing children, favor, etc.
- A strong biblical undergirding leading to righteous living.
- Relevant examples to show us how these principles work.
- Rather than easy fixes, promoting a God-pleasing lifestyle.
- Rather than merely giving us principles, prescribing the "how-to."

It is my honor to recommend this book. For many, it will be the key to the freedom they have been yearning for. Let the swelling subside, and let the windows swing wide open.

—Dr. Samuel R. Chand

★ ★ ★ ★ ★

PART 1

[25 THINGS THAT WILL CLOSE THE WINDOWS OF HEAVEN]

★ ★ ★ ★ ★

★ ★ ★ ★ ★

REASON #1—NOT TITHING

AS YOU JOURNEY THROUGH THIS BOOK, YOU will find that there are many things we can do to either open or close the windows of heaven in our finances. Face it: finances are a part of all of our lives on a daily basis; and the Bible says more about our finances than any other topic in the Bible. With that in mind, we must be assured that God does care about our finances, and that He wants us as His children to prosper. Remember, though, how 3 John 1:2 concludes: "Even as our soul prospers."

The first reason the windows of heaven will close in your financial life is for not tithing. I know what is going through many of your minds at this moment, within the first few seconds of picking up this book. You're thinking, "I can't even pay my bills; that's why I wanted to study and find out how to get out of this mess! If I pay out another 10%, I will never get ahead." My friend, that is how the enemy is holding you back. He knows that, as long as you see what you have as being yours, you can never advance financially. Granted, you may already be in over your head; so what do you have to lose? Let me share with you a personal testimony:

When I moved to Atlanta and began to attend Bible college, the Lord truly blessed me with a great job. At the age of nineteen, I was managing a pretty large wholesale grocery store. The pay was excellent, but to be honest with you, I was young and had many needs. I was paying my way through college, had my own car payments, had to pay room and board, and was dating my future wife. I just didn't have the money left over to pay "tithes." The farther I went in life, the farther into debt I fell. I just couldn't get ahead—even working overtime, I was somehow spending more than I was making. Truly, my pockets had holes in them, and the money was going out much more quickly than it was coming in.

I grew discouraged. I'd heard that God wanted to bless me if I gave Him what belonged to Him. But I was making pretty good money! *Do you know how much 10% is?* I thought. I would be tithing almost $100 per week—for a young man in the 80s, that was a lot of money. I never got there; I just couldn't take that plunge. Finally, God had to show me that He was going to get it, one way or another. I could either give it willingly, or He could use other means of taking it from me. God will not be robbed.

As time went on, I tried to reason with Him and "bless" Him with a ten instead of a dollar every now and then, but God was not impressed. Within a week, I was robbed at my business six times. The last time was with a sawed-off shotgun held to my head, and I couldn't get the safe open for the robber. His voice still rings in my ears: "This is your last chance." I could not remember the combination; but somehow, when I jerked on the door, it swung open, and I knew that God Himself had opened it for me.

That night, I quit that great job. God eventually promoted me into ministry, making $50 per week. It was then that I knew I had to give God his $5 per week. Isn't that amazing? I couldn't give God $100 when I was making $1,000, but now that I was making $50, I could give Him $5. The truth is, I knew that, if God didn't bless the $50, life was over for me.

I want you to understand something: you don't know until you are taught. That is why Sister Joyce and I are co-authoring this book. We want your eyes to be opened. I was in ministry and didn't believe in tithing. God had to bring me down a few notches and let me know that He was the source of my life, my health, and my finances. If you think you can do it on your own, you're only kidding yourself.

Let's take a look at Malachi 3:10 (KJV): "Prove me now herewith … if I will not open you the window of heaven…" Those who do not are under a curse. Malachi 3:9 says, "Ye are cursed with a curse." If you are wondering if God would curse you as a Christian, take a look at Ananias and Sapphira in Acts 5.

Now a man named Ananias, together with his wife Sapphira, also sold a piece of property. With his wife's full knowledge he kept back part of the money for himself, but brought the rest and put it at the apostles' feet.

Then Peter said, "Ananias, how is it that Satan has so filled your heart that you have lied to the Holy Spirit and have kept for yourself some of the money you received for the land? Didn't it belong to you before it was sold? And after it was sold, wasn't the money at your disposal? What made you think of doing such a thing? You have not lied just to human beings but to God."

When Ananias heard this, he fell down and died. And great fear seized all who heard what had happened. Then some young men came forward, wrapped up his body, and carried him out and buried him.

About three hours later his wife came in, not knowing what had happened. Peter asked her, "Tell me, is this the price you and Ananias got for the land?"

"Yes," she said, "that is the price."

Peter said to her, "How could you conspire to test the Spirit of the Lord? Listen! The feet of the men who buried your husband are at the door, and they will carry you out also."

At that moment she fell down at his feet and died. Then the young men came in and, finding her dead, carried her out and buried her beside her husband (Acts 5:1-10).

Ananias and Sapphira had violated a spiritual principle. Lying is a sin. The Bible is clear: "For the wages of sin is death" (Romans 6:23). Their disobedience brought about their deaths. "The one who sins is the one who will die" (Ezekiel 18:4). Ananias and Sapphira lied, so they died.

When did the curse of death as a result of sin begin? It began at the beginning with Adam and Eve. Adam and Eve worked. They had a job. Their job was to tend the garden. Genesis 2:15 tells us, "The LORD God took the man and put him in the Garden of Eden to work it and take care of it." In addition to working, Adam and Eve received pay. In return for working the garden, God allowed them to eat freely of every tree.

This concept of work and wages occurs in the New Testament also. The Apostle Paul, in 1 Corinthians 9:7, asks, "Who serves as a soldier at his own expense? Who plants a vineyard and does not eat of its grapes? Who tends a flock and does not drink of the milk?" There was no exception to this rule in the Garden of Eden. Genesis 2:16 makes this clear: "And the LORD God commanded the man, 'You are free to eat from any tree in the garden…'"

However, God had a right to Adam and Eve's harvest. He placed an important restriction on their harvest: He forbade Adam and Eve from eating from one certain tree. They were to bestow their labor on it, just as they did on every other tree, but they could not eat any of its fruit. In the next verse, God says, "'But you must not eat from the tree of the knowledge of good and evil, for when you eat of it you will surely die.'" This was Adam and Eve's tithe, and it foreshadowed the concept which would become part of the Law of Moses: "A tithe of everything from the land, whether grain from the soil or fruit from the trees, belongs to the LORD; it is holy to the LORD" (Leviticus 27:30).

Not only did disobedience regarding tithing cause a big problem in the Garden of Eden, but it also played a big part in the conflict between Cain and Abel: "And Abel also brought an offering—fat portions from some of the firstborn of his flock. The LORD looked with favor on Abel and his offering..." (Genesis 4:4). Jealousy over this tithe-induced favor led to the world's first murder.

Abraham was a tither. In Genesis 14:19-20, after Melchizedek, Priest of God Most High, pronounced, "Blessed be Abram by God Most High, Creator of heaven and earth. And praise be to God Most High, who delivered your enemies into your hand," the Scripture says that "Abram gave him a tenth of everything."

In Matthew 23:23, Jesus personally endorsed tithing. "Woe to you, teachers of the law and Pharisees, you hypocrites! You give a tenth of your spices—mint, dill and cumin. But you have neglected the more important matters of the law—justice, mercy and faithfulness. You should have practiced the latter, without neglecting the former."

Not tithing costs the saints—not God!

★ ★ ★ ★ ★

REASON #2—WRONG PRIORITIES

S ALVATION CAUSES US TO SHED THE OLD nature of the first
Adam and put on the new nature of the second Adam, who is
Jesus! We see this in Ephesians 4:22-24: "You were taught, with
regard to your former way of life, to put off your old self, which is
being corrupted by its deceitful desires; to be made new in the attitude of your minds; and to put on the new self, created to be like God
in true righteousness and holiness."

God cares about us! And He knows us so well that He is not
surprised by the tension we feel regarding meeting our own needs.
That's why, beginning in verse 25 of the above passage, our Lord
focuses on the things we will eat, drink, and wear. He brings to our
attention how He cares for the birds and flowers. He shows us how
well He supplies for them from His open heaven. Then, He declares
how much more He desires to supply all of our needs.

Furthermore, in Matthew 6:30, Jesus tells his followers, "'If
that is how God clothes the grass of the field, which is here today
and tomorrow is thrown into the fire, will he not much more clothe

you— you of little faith?'" In the next two verses, He tells them not to worry about these necessities of life. He says that worrying and seeking after basic needs is the way the children of darkness live. It is definitely not the way we should occupy our time.

PRIORITIES

Is Jesus really all we need? Matthew 6:32 says that our Heavenly Father knows "that you need [all these things]." However, they pale in comparison to our need for Christ. The Apostle Paul was so much attuned to the necessity of making Jesus his Lord that he kept a constant vigil over his flesh to keep it under the rulership of Christ.

Paul asks the church in Corinth, "Do you not know that in a race all the runners run, but only one gets the prize? Run in such a way as to get the prize. Everyone who competes in the games goes into strict training. They do it to get a crown that will not last; but we do it to get a crown that will last forever. Therefore I do not run like someone running aimlessly; I do not fight like a boxer beating the air. No, I strike a blow to my body and make it my slave so that after I have preached to others, I myself will not be disqualified for the prize" (1 Corinthians 9:24-27).

Paul recognized the constant effort it took to lay hold of the Kingdom of God. He also knew that, if he did not work at it, he would not be able to receive all he needed through an open heaven. Hear the great apostle's conclusion of what could happen to him if he didn't do his best: In 1 Corinthians 9:27, he confesses, "No, I strike a blow to my body and make it my slave so that after I have preached to others, I myself will not be disqualified for the prize."

Whatever you do, don't stop seeking first the Kingdom of God. Don't stop putting first the active pursuit of Jesus Christ as your total Lord and Master. For if you stop, the windows of heaven will close over your life, and all the things you need will stop being added to you.

Just as you've trusted Him for your salvation, commit your daily life and needs to his care as you live a crucified life. Consider Galatians 2:20: "I have been crucified with Christ and I no longer live, but

Christ lives in me. The life I now live in the body, I live by faith in the Son of God, who loved me and gave himself for me."

1 Peter 2:9 says, "But you are a chosen people, a royal priesthood, a holy nation, God's special possession, that you may declare the praises of him who called you out of darkness into his wonderful light."

And Ephesians 5:1 says, "Follow God's example, therefore, as dearly loved children."

★ ★ ★ ★ ★

REASON #3—DOUBLE-MINDEDNESS

THE BIBLE STATES THAT UNDECIDED, DOUBTING PEOPLE cannot receive from God. What should the person who doubts, when he or she has asked God for wisdom, expect to receive? "That person should not expect to receive anything from the Lord. Such a person is double-minded and unstable in all they do" (James 1:7-8).

Matthew 21:28-31 describes this situation applied to real action: "'What do you think? There was a man who had two sons. He went to the first and said, "Son, go and work today in the vineyard." "I will not," he answered, but later he changed his mind and went. Then the father went to the other son and said the same thing. He answered, "I will, sir," but he did not go. Which of the two did what his father wanted?' 'The first,' they answered. Jesus said to them, 'Truly I tell you, the tax collectors and the prostitutes are entering the kingdom of God ahead of you.'"

Look at it like this: Everyone has two minds. A person's sub-conscious mind keeps up with every detail of the many functions the human body must perform, whereas a person's conscious mind tends to be lazy. It can compromise, lie, distort, and be constantly at odds with the subconscious mind. While the conscious mind can be quite comfortable with a lie or half-truth, the subconscious mind reacts against anything it hears that's different from what it believes to be true.

What is a double-minded Christian? A double-minded Christian is one who has two conflicting opinions or desires taking place in his two minds about the same subject. This disagreement between the two minds is common in Christians. It is especially common in those who do not regularly study the Word of God. Regular Bible study is absolutely necessary if you want your two minds to stay in agreement with each other. 2 Timothy 2:15 advises the Christian as to why this is so important: "Do your best to present yourself to God as one approved, a worker who does not need to be ashamed and who correctly handles the word of truth."

Believers must decide if God wants them to be sick or well, rich or poor, growing or dying. Based on what you know and believe about the character of God, choose, so that you don't exhibit double-mindedness. Otherwise, one day, you are happy and excited, while the next day, you are discouraged and depressed.

According to Hebrews 4:12, the Word of God has the power to help you: "For the word of God is living and active. Sharper than any double-edged sword, it penetrates even to dividing soul and spirit, joints and marrow; it judges the thoughts and attitudes of the heart." Trust that, whichever choice you make, God's Word will lead you to a proper mindset, and doubt will be unnecessary.

★ ★ ★ ★ ★

REASON #4—UNACCEPTED OFFERINGS

GOD DOES NOT HAVE TO ACCEPT YOUR offering. For instance, He will not receive a gift given in disobedience, or a gift from someone who wants to receive something against His will. Most people never give any thought to whether or not God accepts their offerings. If you just think about it a moment, you will realize that, if He doesn't accept your offering, God is not obligated to multiply it back to you.

It's clear that God does not always accept our gifts. Amos 5:22 describes one such situation: "Even though you bring me burnt offerings and grain offerings, I will not accept them. Though you bring choice fellowship offerings, I will have no regard for them." Malachi 1:10 illustrates another: "'Oh, that one of you would shut the temple doors, so that you would not light useless fires on my altar! I am not pleased with you,' says the LORD Almighty, 'and I will accept no offering from your hands.'"

Keep in mind that your church will accept any offering placed in the offering plate. It doesn't matter if it's a penny or a million dollars.

However, your church doesn't promise to multiply back the money you give to it. So, if you plan to receive anything back from your offering, you must give it in such a way that God will accept it.

The first step in having God accept your offering is to be sure that you give it with a willing mind. Remember, God prizes the cheerful givers; those who give grudgingly or unwillingly are displeasing to Him. If you have trouble giving joyfully, it is doubtful that God will accept your offering, as stated in 2 Corinthians 9:7: "Each of you should give what you have decided in your heart to give, not reluctantly or under compulsion, for God loves a cheerful giver."

The second step in giving an acceptable offering is to give according to what you have. The key word in this requirement is the word "according." You must give your offering according to the things God has already given you. This speaks of those things you now possess: "For if the willingness is there, the gift is acceptable according to what one has, not according to what he does not have" (2 Corinthians 8:12).

In both of these steps, the amount you give is not as important to God as your motivation in giving it. When the things He has already given to you guide you in your giving, you will be motivated by gratitude. God will be sure to accept your offering when your heart is stirred to give because of His goodness to you.

Keep in mind, though, that tithes and offerings are viewed differently. A tithe is not the property of the giver; it is the property of the Lord. It is also not an amount the giver decides. God has determined the amount of a tithe to be 10 percent. An offering is always a gift given to the Lord, and begins only after you pay the tithe.

When considering giving an offering, you may ask, "How much should I give?" Scripture allows you to determine the amount. You may give whatever you've decided in your heart, within the limits of your cheerfulness and single-mindedness. But remember this: If your offering doesn't move you, it won't move God.

★ ★ ★ ★ ★

REASON #5—NOT UNDERSTANDING

MANY NEW CONVERTS DO NOT UNDERSTAND THE principle of tithing. This personal note from Karen Green illustrates a situation like this:

> Growing up in a small conservative Baptist church, I was never taught the principles of tithing or of sowing and reaping. It wasn't until I moved to Georgia and became a member of Living Faith Tabernacle that I began to learn of God's principle of tithing. In the three years that I have been a member, I have learned through Pastor Chris's sermons and the in-depth study of God's Word just what the Lord requires of us. I have found that, in order for God to bless us, He requires us to be obedient to Him. If you are faithful to Him, He will be faithful to you. I've experienced this first-hand in my life.
>
> I have gone through many trials since moving to Georgia, but through them all, God has been faithful to me. He has brought me through two major surgeries this past year within

a five-month period, with complete healing in my body. I give Him all the praise, honor and glory for this. My doctor was astounded at how quickly I recuperated, and I know it was because of the awesome favor I have with my Heavenly Father. In addition, He has also blessed my life with wonderful friends here, a loving church family, a great job which allows me to work from home most of the time, and great health. God wants us to have an abundant life and walk in His blessings, but He first requires us to be faithful to Him and give Him what is His.

The Bible tells us that God's people perish for lack of knowledge—and not being taught about God's principles of tithing all those years is a perfect example of that. I thank God that He placed me here under the authority of Pastor Chris so that I could learn about all the benefits God has for my life.

I will always give to God what is His because I know that, when I do this, He will bless me abundantly, as He will bless anyone else who is simply obedient to Him.

Matthew 13:23 says, "But the seed falling on good soil refers to someone who hears the word and understands it. This is the one who produces a crop, yielding a hundred, sixty or thirty times what was sown." This is a most fitting description of Karen and others whose hearts were prepared for sowing and reaping through proper teaching.

Teachers and students of the Word should keep three powerful Scriptures in mind: the first is Mark 4:23-25, which says, "'If anyone has ears to hear, let them hear. Consider carefully what you hear,' he continued. 'With the measure you use, it will be measured to you—and even more. Whoever has will be given more; whoever does not have, even what he has will be taken from him.'"

Focus on hearing. The Greek word *akouo* means "to hear with understanding," as demonstrated in Matthew 15:10: "Jesus called the crowd to him and said, 'Listen and understand.'"

What you hear can hurt you spiritually. You must be careful who you allow to teach you. Matthew 15:14, which says, "If the blind leads the blind, both will fall into a pit," goes hand-in-hand with this idea. Jesus told the scribes and Pharisees that they were teaching the people wrongly. He went on to say that, because of this wrong teaching, the people were no longer able to receive the truth. Finally, He concluded that false teachers cannot properly lead the people. If they try, it will be disastrous for both the teacher and the students.

The one who teaches you the Word of God will mold your understanding of it. What you learn from your teacher is what you will understand. What your pastor or teacher understands will either help or hinder your ability to receive from God. We can see the proof of these facts as we look further into the words Jesus spoke in Mark 4:24 (KJV): "With what measure (of understanding) ye mete (do your giving), it (that which you receive) shall be measured to you again."

Jesus said that whatever measure of understanding you have when you give affects your ability to receive—it will either be expanded or it will be limited to the extent of your understanding. If you understand little, you will receive little. If you understand much, you will receive much. The more you understand, the more you can receive.

3 John 2 gives us more insight into the importance of properly understanding in order to receive health and prosperity: "Dear friend, I pray that you may enjoy good health and that all may go well with you, even as your soul is getting along well." Let me paraphrase this: "Beloved, I pray above all that you might prosper and be in health, even as your understanding increases."

If you notice, the foremost prayer of the Apostle John was that his readers prosper and be in health, for he said that he prayed for these things above all others. However, he placed a condition on whether or not they would be able to receive health and prosperity. The condition was that their souls (and ours) must prosper. The book of 2 Peter repeats this same truth in 2 Peter 1:3 (KJV): "His divine power hath given unto us all things that pertain unto life and godliness, through the knowledge of him." Peter is saying that our Lord will provide everything we need for all areas of life. However, there is a condition: what we need can come to us only through the knowledge (understanding) of Him (Jesus).

Scripture shows us God's willingness to bless us and give us all sufficiency. Most Christians cannot grasp that these verses mean exactly what they say. Look at Proverbs 10:22 (KJV) afresh and anew: "The blessing of the Lord, it maketh rich, and he addeth no sorrow with it."

Hear and understand that God wants to bless you by making you rich. However, notice that He wants to bring riches to you in such a way that you will have no sorrow from them. If you understand this verse, it becomes possible for you to receive those riches. But if you mistakenly understand that God wants you to be poor, you can't receive wealth from Him.

Romans 8:32 (KJV) attests that "He that spared not his own Son, but delivered him up for us all, how shall he not with him also freely give us all things?" Understand that God already gave it all to you when He gave Jesus for you. He has already given His most precious possession. Now, take a moment and let that thought sink in. If He has already given His most precious possession for you, why would He now refuse to give you the things you need?

Once you understand how precious His Son is to Him, then you will be able to understand that He will withhold nothing from you. But your understanding always limits your ability to receive from God. John 8:32 (KJV) simply states, "And ye shall know the truth, and the truth shall make you free." Understanding the truth is critical. How does that happen? A young King Solomon shows us.

> At Gibeon the LORD appeared to Solomon during the night in a dream, and God said, "Ask for whatever you want me to give you."
>
> Solomon answered, "You have shown great kindness to your servant, my father David, because he was faithful to you and righteous and upright in heart. You have continued

this great kindness to him and have given him a son to sit on his throne this very day.

Now, LORD my God, you have made your servant king in place of my father David. But I am only a little child and do not know how to carry out my duties. Your servant is here among the people you have chosen, a great people, too numerous to count or number. So give your servant a discerning heart to govern your people and to distinguish between right and wrong. For who is able to govern this great people of yours?"

The Lord was pleased that Solomon had asked for this. So God said to him, "Since you have asked for this and not for long life or wealth for yourself, nor have asked for the death of your enemies but for discernment in administering justice, I will do what you have asked. I will give you a wise and discerning heart, so that there will never have been anyone like you, nor will there ever be. Moreover, I will give you what you have not asked for—both wealth and honor—so that in your lifetime you will have no equal among kings. And if you walk in obedience to me and keep my decrees and commands as David your father did, I will give you a long life" (1 Kings 3:5-14).

HOW TO RECEIVE UNDERSTANDING

Seek the Lord—Proverbs 28:5 says, "Evildoers do not understand what is right, but those who seek the LORD understand it fully."

Shun evil—Daniel 12:10 says, "Many will be purified, made spotless and refined, but the wicked will continue to be wicked. None of the wicked will understand, but those who are wise will understand."

Walk in faith—Hebrews 11:1-3 says, "Now faith is confidence in what we hope for and assurance about what we do not see. This is what the ancients were commended for. By faith we understand that the universe was formed at God's command, so that what is seen was not made out of what was visible." And Romans 10:17 says,

"Consequently, faith comes from hearing the message, and the message is heard through the word about Christ."

Study the Word of God—2 Timothy 2:15 says, "Do your best to present yourself to God as one approved, a worker who does not need to be ashamed and who correctly handles the word of truth."

Pray like an apostle—Ephesians 1:15-17 says, "For this reason, ever since I heard about your faith in the Lord Jesus and your love for all God's people, I have not stopped giving thanks for you, remembering you in my prayers. I keep asking that the God of our Lord Jesus Christ, the glorious Father, may give you the Spirit of wisdom and revelation, so that you may know him better."

★ ★ ★ ★ ★

REASON #6—FEAR

A QUICK READING OF THE FIRST 33 VERSES of the Book of Job will reveal that every bad thing you can imagine happened to Job. Sabeans stole his herds of oxen and asses (1:14-15), lightning burned up his sheep and servants (1:16), Chaldeans robbed him of his camels (1:17), a tornado blew down the house and killed his sons and daughters (1:18), and grievous boils covered his body (2:17). If those weren't enough, his wife encouraged him to curse his God and die (2:9). The final blow came when his friends came over and began to accuse him (2:11).

It is important for you to notice that, of all the emotions God gave Job, fear was not one of them. 2 Timothy 1:7 (KJV) says, "For God hath not given us the spirit of fear; but of power, and of love, and of a sound mind." The spirit of fear does not come from God!

Fear acts as a magnet. As amazing as it may seem, fear actually helps make the thing you are afraid of happen. Jesus understood this principle. That is why He always blocked fear.

Fear tried to take over as He was going to the house of the young ruler to heal the man's daughter. While they were en route, news came to them that the little girl had died. According to Luke 8:49,

"While Jesus was still speaking, someone came from the house of Jairus, the synagogue leader. 'Your daughter is dead,' he said. 'Don't bother the teacher anymore.'"

Notice how quickly our Lord blocked fear. The very next verse says, "Hearing this, Jesus said to Jairus, 'Don't be afraid; just believe, and she will be healed.'" Jesus understood that fear opens a person's life to the devil's control. It gives Satan the opportunity to take your possessions and other beloved things from you. When you allow fear into your life, the windows of heaven close.

It's important to remember that you have nothing to fear because the evil one does not stand a chance against you. You have God in you and with you at all times, as evidenced in 1 John 4:4—"The one who is in you is greater than the one who is in the world"—and 2 Timothy 1:12: "Because I know whom I have believed, and am convinced that he is able to guard what I have entrusted to him until that day." The person who experiences the presence of God has nothing to fear.

Seven kinds of fear are especially common and exceedingly powerful:

The fear of the unknown—John 16:33 says, "I have told you these things, so that in me you may have peace. In this world you will have trouble. But take heart! I have overcome the world."

The fear of death—Psalms 23:4 says, "Even though I walk through the darkest valley, I will fear no evil, for you are with me; your rod and your staff, they comfort me." In addition, Hebrews 2:14-15 says, "Since the children have flesh and blood, he too shared in their humanity so that by his death he might break the power of him who holds the power of death—that is, the devil—and free those who all their lives were held in slavery by their fear of death." Lastly, 1 Corinthians 15:55-57 says, "'Where, O death, is your victory? Where, O death, is your sting?' The sting of death is sin, and the power of sin is the law. But thanks be to God! He gives us the victory through our Lord Jesus Christ."

The fear of man—Proverbs 29:25 says, "Fear of man will prove to be a snare, but whoever trusts in the LORD is kept safe." And Hebrews 13:5-6 says, "Keep your lives free from the love of money and be content with what you have, because God has said, 'Never will I leave you; never will I forsake you.' So we say with confidence, 'The Lord is my helper; I will not be afraid. What can mere mortals do to me?'"

The fear of failure—2 Corinthians 2:14 says, "But thanks be to God, who always leads us as captives in Christ's triumphal procession in Christ and uses us to spread the aroma of the knowledge of him everywhere." In addition, Romans 8:37-39 says, "No, in all these things we are more than conquerors through him who loved us. For I am convinced that neither death nor life, neither angels nor demons, neither the present nor the future, nor any powers, neither height nor depth, nor anything else in all creation, will be able to separate us from the love of God that is in Christ Jesus our Lord."

The fear of rejection—John 6:37 says, "All those the Father gives me will come to me, and whoever comes to me I will never drive away."

The fear of sickness—Isaiah 53:5 says, "But he was pierced for our transgressions, he was crushed for our iniquities; the punishment that brought us peace was on him, and by his wounds we are healed." And Mark 16:17-18 says, "And these signs will accompany those who believe: In my name they will drive out demons; they will speak in new tongues; they will pick up snakes with their hands; and when they drink deadly poison, it will not hurt them at all; they will place their hands on sick people, and they will get well."

The fear of insufficiency—2 Peter 1:3 says, "His divine power has given us everything we need for life and godliness through our knowledge of him who called us by his own glory and goodness." In addition, Romans 8:32 says, "He who did not spare his own Son, but gave him up for us all—how will he not also, along with him, graciously give us all things?" Lastly, Ecclesiastes 5:18-19 says, "This is what I have observed to be good: that it is appropriate for a person to eat, to drink and to find satisfaction in their toilsome labor under the sun during the few days of life God has given them—for this is their lot. Moreover, when God gives someone wealth and possessions, and the ability to enjoy them, to accept their lot and be happy in their toil—this is a gift of God."

Don't let fear of any kind come near you. If it does, cast it down in the strong name of Jesus. 2 Timothy 1:7 (KJV) makes it clear that fear does not come from God, but rather from the evil one: "For God hath not given us the spirit of fear." It is a Biblical fact that fear closes the windows of heaven. It brings no good thing with it; in fact, it draws only bad things to you. Fear is not part of God's plan for you. Take to heart Jesus' words in Luke 12:32: "Do not be afraid…for your Father has been pleased to give you the kingdom." Resist fear, and watch the windows of heaven open over your life.

REASON #7—NO FAITH

I F THE WORD OF GOD IS CLEAR about anything, it is that God expects His children to live by faith! Romans 1:17 testifies to this: "For in the gospel the righteousness from God is revealed—a righteousness that is by faith from first to last, just as it is written: 'The righteous will live by faith.'" And if you're not sure what faith is, Hebrews 11:1 explains, "Now faith is confidence in what we hope for and assurance about what we do not see."

We also receive by faith. Matthew 9:27 (KJV) describes two blind men calling out to Jesus, "Thou Son of David, have mercy on us." In verse 29 (NIV), "He touched their eyes and said, 'According to your faith let it be done to you.'" With these powerful words of instruction, our Lord declared the important part their faith played in receiving from Him. Jesus went directly to the root of their problem: they needed faith to be healed. Jesus told the two blind men they would find healing for their blindness according to their faith.

Lack of faith closes the windows of heaven: according to Hebrews 11:6, "Without faith it is impossible to please God, because anyone who comes to him must believe that he exists and that he rewards those who earnestly seek him." Think about it: heaven does not open over a person with whom God is not pleased.

It's not uncommon to wonder how a person can receive faith. God's Word says He will give it to you in Romans 12:3: "For by the grace given me I say to every one of you: Do not think of yourself more highly than you ought, but rather think of yourself with sober judgment, in accordance with the measure of faith God has given you." Notice that, according to this verse, God doesn't give the measure of faith to everyone. He gives it to everyone who is among us— those born again. Once you are saved, you receive the measure of faith. It then becomes absolutely necessary for you to get into God's Word so that your faith can increase. Romans 10:17 explains, "Consequently, faith comes from hearing the message, and the message is heard through the word about Christ."

Then, as your knowledge of Scripture grows, Hebrews 12:2 describes how Jesus will develop strong faith in you even to perfection: "Fixing our eyes on Jesus, the author and perfecter of our faith. For the joy set before him he endured the cross, scorning its shame, and sat down at the right hand of the throne of God." As the Author and Perfecter of faith, Jesus is the only one who can do it.

★ ★ ★ ★ ★

REASON #8—UNBELIEF

MANY TIMES, THE WINDOWS OF BLESSING IN our lives close due to our lack of belief. Merium Leverett shares this in the personal testimony of her experience as a young Christian:

Being a new Christian, there is so much to learn. Tithing was one of those things I had to learn the hard way. When I first gave my heart to the Lord, I was so excited; I wanted to do everything I could to please the Lord—except turn loose my money. I didn't mind giving my ten or twenty dollars on Sunday morning, but the thought of giving the Lord 10% of our salaries was just not right. How in the world would we make it? We had three children to provide for, and there was simply no way I could turn loose ten percent of our salaries. At that time, it would make my offerings go from $20 on a good day to $50, $60, maybe even $70 a week. We struggled for every dime we received.

Then one Saturday night, as we were going over our bills and trying to figure out how to "rob Peter to pay Paul," my husband told me he felt we needed to start tithing properly.

He was raised in church. He understood the principles of tithing, although it had been years since he attended church and tithed. I was not raised in church, and I did not want to hear that I had to add yet another "bill" to the pile. In a heated argument, I told him, "Fine, I will pay ten percent for one month, and you will see just how broke we really are."

The next day, I went into church and gave our 10%. Every Sunday for one month, I gave our tithe. At the end of the month, all the bills were paid, our tithe was paid, and we even had a few dollars left in the bank. To this day, I can only say that God provided, because we honestly did not have enough money to make ends meet. From that day forward, my UNBELIEF turned to BELIEF! I started sharing my new-found knowledge with everyone I knew. I did not believe that we could afford another "bill," but I found out very quickly that we couldn't afford to NOT pay our tithes.

Merium's experience is proof of Matthew 13:58, which says, "And he did not do many miracles there because of their lack of faith." If she and her husband had not decided to tithe, the Lord never would have done the miracle of expanding their finances to meet all their needs. Continued unbelief would have meant continued barely-paid bills.

Unbelief doesn't only affect unbelievers. Many times, unbelief involves believers. When the children of God walk in unbelief, it is usually only for a season. This situation is different from being an unbeliever, for unbelievers constantly walk in unbelief. John the Baptist, whose account is chronicled in John 1:29-32, was obviously a believer, and yet he still experienced unbelief.

"The next day John saw Jesus coming toward him and said, 'Look, the Lamb of God, who takes away the sin of the world! This is the one I meant when I said, "A man who comes after me has surpassed me because he was before me." I myself did not know him, but the reason I came baptizing with water was that he might be revealed to Israel.' Then John gave this testimony: 'I saw the Spirit come down from heaven as a dove and remain on him.'"

There is no doubt about it. At this point, John the Baptist had faith. If anyone believed in Jesus, he did! However, fear affects faith. After many days and nights in the dungeon, something happened to John the Baptist. Unbelief began to take over his mind. Listen to how his words changed after the plow of fear had done its work: Matthew 11:2-3 says, "When John, who was in prison, heard about the deeds of the Messiah, he sent his disciples to ask him, 'Are you the one who is to come, or should we expect someone else?'"

I don't believe for a moment that this giant of a man suddenly became an unbeliever. He simply gave way to unbelief for a season. Jesus responded by sending John's messengers back to him. He told them to tell John again those things He was doing in Matthew 11:11: "Truly I tell you, Among those born of women there has not risen anyone greater than John the Baptist; yet whoever is least in the kingdom of heaven is greater than he."

When we talked about fear earlier, we talked about Mark chapter 5, in which Jairus approached Jesus, and Jesus agreed to heal his daughter. As they went toward the house, the woman with the issue of blood saw Jesus and touched the hem of his garment. Jesus spent precious moments ministering to her. How this delay must have troubled Jairus! If this woman had not interrupted them, they would already be at his daughter's side, and Jesus would be ministering to her. No doubt fear began to arise when Jairus saw those familiar faces approaching. Jesus recognized it, and told him not to allow unbelief to have any place in his thinking. He told Jairus to believe only, for Jesus knew that unbelief—left unchallenged—would soon chase belief away.

The Apostle Peter allowed himself to be temporarily disconnected from his faith. As you know, unbelief stopped his famous walk on the water. Scripture doesn't say he was going to walk on the water. Matthew 14:29-31 says, "'Come,' he said. Then Peter got down out of the boat, walked on the water and came toward Jesus." Then, as quickly as the miracle began, unbelief entered his mind, and it ended: "But when he saw the wind, he was afraid and, beginning to sink, cried out, 'Lord, save me!' Immediately Jesus reached out his hand and caught him. 'You of little faith,' he said, 'why did you doubt?'"

In 2 Corinthians 10:4-5, we are told how to combat unbelief: "The weapons we fight with are not the weapons of the world. On the contrary, they have divine power to demolish strongholds. We demolish arguments and every pretension that sets itself up against the knowledge of God, and we take captive every thought to make it obedient to Christ."

We can see the full meaning of this verse in the Amplified translation, and we must take it to heart: "The weapons of our warfare are not physical [weapons of flesh and blood]. Our weapons are divinely powerful for the destruction of fortresses. We are destroying sophisticated arguments and every exalted and proud thing that sets itself up against the [true] knowledge of God, and we are taking every thought and purpose captive to the obedience of Christ, "

REASON #9—WRONG DESIRES

WHOSE DESIRES ARE YOU TRYING TO FULFILL? Are they yours or the Lord's? Psalm 37:4 instructs, "Take delight in the Lord, and he will give you the desires of your heart." When you seek to fulfill only your own desires, you make it impossible for Jesus to accomplish His purpose in your life.

When we find ourselves not receiving the things we are asking for, maybe it's time for a self-evaluation. Jesus tells us in Matthew 6:33, "But seek first his kingdom and his righteousness, and all these things will be given to you as well." Jesus is telling us not to worry about food, clothing, and shelter, because our Heavenly Father knows we need these things. What goes wrong in our lives, so often, is that we desire more than the "necessities" in life. We want to live beyond our means.

When we are truly seeking God's will for us above everything else, we will find blessings in every area—finances, physical health, relationships, and so on. But when our priorities are out of alignment, we tie God's hands. I have often said that God cannot allow many Christians to obtain wealth because He knows what they would do with it. Money doesn't change people, as it is often accused of doing— it actually brings out their true personalities!

Make a list of what you would do if you were to suddenly come into a large amount of money. Then, look at that list and honestly assess it. Does it line up with what God would be pleased with, or is it full of selfish desires?

Jesus is the perfect pattern; if you want to know how to be pleasing to the Father, Jesus is the only example to follow. Determine what Jesus would do in any given circumstance, and you will know what you should do. Jesus made an important statement for anyone who wishes to please the Father. He said, "By myself I can do nothing; I judge only as I hear, and my judgment is just, for I seek not to please myself but him who sent me" (John 5:30). He never did what He wanted to do; He did only those things the Father wanted Him to do.

A person's wrong desires can close heaven. James 4:2 describes this: "You desire but do not have, so you kill. You covet but you cannot get what you want, so you quarrel and fight. You do not have because you do not ask God."

Notice three key words in that verse: covet, kill, and desire. Each speaks of a person's own will. Notice how any one of these three things is able to stop you from receiving from God. God says that longing for your own desires will cause you to not have them. The problem is not that you have desires; the problem is longing for what you want instead of what God wants for you.

But there is good news: God can make your desires right. Be soft and pliable in the hand of God, and He will give you new desires. Roll over onto Him the responsibility of deciding which way you should go. Put your trust in Him, and He will bring to pass the new desires He's able to put in your heart because of your willingness to let go of your old ones.

★ ★ ★ ★ ★

REASON #10—LOOKING BACK

SOME PEOPLE FIND FASCINATION IN THEIR FORMER sins. Without realizing it, this fascination holds them back from progressing in their Christian walks. However, God's Word tells us plainly what He thinks about us dwelling on the past. In Luke 9:62, Jesus replied, "No one who puts a hand to the plow and looks back is fit for service in the kingdom of God."

Many of us are merely enduring instead of enjoying. Christians find themselves looking back with longing to their old lives of fun and adventure, forgetting the misery that went along with them. They see their new lives in Christ as merely something to endure until they go to heaven. Christianity did not draw them because of its wonder and glory; they are saved for only one reason: that they might miss hell.

When we look back and see what we've left behind instead of looking forward to see what God has in store for us, we run the risk of facing consequences similar to Lot's wife.

> With the coming of dawn, the angels urged Lot, saying, "Hurry! Take your wife and your two daughters who are here, or you will be swept away when the city is punished."

When he hesitated, the men grasped his hand and the hands of his wife and of his two daughters and led them safely out of the city, for the LORD was merciful to them. As soon as they had brought them out, one of them said, "Flee for your lives! Don't look back, and don't stop anywhere in the plain! Flee to the mountains or you will be swept away!"

But Lot said to them, "No, my lords, please! Your servant has found favor in your eyes, and you have shown great kindness to me in sparing my life. But I can't flee to the mountains; this disaster will overtake me, and I'll die. Look, here is a town near enough to run to, and it is small. Let me flee to it—it is very small, isn't it? Then my life will be spared."

He said to him, "Very well, I will grant this request too; I will not overthrow the town you speak of. But flee there quickly, because I cannot do anything until you reach it." (That is why the town was called Zoar.)

By the time Lot reached Zoar, the sun had risen over the land. Then the LORD rained down burning sulfur on Sodom and Gomorrah—from the LORD out of the heavens. Thus he overthrew those cities and the entire plain, destroying all those living in the cities—and also the vegetation in the land. But Lot's wife looked back, and she became a pillar of salt. (Genesis 19:15-26)

Even New Testament believers were tempted and gave in to the temptation of looking back. Paul laments, "For Demas, because he loved this world, has deserted me and has gone to Thessalonica," (2 Timothy 4:10).

Looking back is not inevitable, though! Describing his own walk in Philippians 3:13-14, Paul says, "Brothers and sisters, I do not consider myself yet to have taken hold of it. But one thing I do: Forgetting what is behind and straining toward what is ahead, I press on toward the goal to win the prize for which God has called me heavenward in Christ Jesus."

As long as your Christianity remains in neutral, the things of this world are going to be more interesting to you than the things of the Christ-life. And if you don't press toward the mark of the high calling of Christ, there is a definite possibility that you will begin to look back with longing to the old life. You will become unfit for the Kingdom of God.

Both the Old Testament and the New coach us on how to keep our eyes focused toward the front. Isaiah 43:18-19 reminds, "Forget the former things; do not dwell on the past. See, I am doing a new thing! Now it springs up; do you not perceive it? I am making a way in the desert and streams in the wasteland." Ephesians 4:22-23 continues, "You were taught, with regard to your former way of life, to put off your old self, which is being corrupted by its deceitful desires; to be made new in the attitude of your minds"

The Bible is equally clear about the reward we can expect as we focus forward. 1 Corinthians 2:9-10 states, "As it is written: 'What no eye has seen, what no ear has heard, and what no human mind has conceived"—the things God has prepared for those who love him— these are the things God has revealed to us by his Spirit. The Spirit searches all things, even the deep things of God." John 14:2-3 adds that Jesus promised, "'My Father's house has many rooms; if that were not so, would I have told you that I am going there to prepare a place for you? 3 And if I go and prepare a place for you, I will come back and take you to be with me that you also may be where I am.'"

If you'll begin to study the Word of God earnestly, you'll find a completely new way to live. The Bible will start you on a bold adventure that will quickly lead you into a lifestyle so much more interesting and satisfying than anything from your past. You won't want to look back—in fact, you will actually be repulsed by the thought of doing so.

·

★ ★ ★ ★ ★

REASON #11—WRONG MARITAL RELATIONSHIPS

FINANCES PLAY A VITAL ROLE IN THE success or failure of a marriage. Here is the personal testimony of Kathy Bowen, relating her own experience:

It is a known fact that the two top causes for divorce are infidelity and money issues. Many couples go into a marriage with the wrong idea about money. The Bible teaches us that marriage is when two people join together and become ONE flesh. A sure sign of distrust and doubt within a couple is when there are separate accounts, and you hear phrases such as, "That's MY money." It's as if the couple went into the relationship with the plan of the marriage failing, so they just keep everything separate to make life easier when the time comes to throw in the towel!

I heard a profound statement when I was younger that I carried into my marriage and have cultivated throughout the years. It is this: "In a strong and lasting relationship, each spouse should try to out-serve the another." This applies to our finances as well as our physical needs. When we don't trust our spouse enough to put our earnings together, I believe we are setting ourselves and our marriages up for failure.

I realize, though, that we must also be honest and know our strengths and weaknesses. If you are the type of person who can't handle money and you tend to spend all that you have, you definitely shouldn't be the one handling the money for your household! God is so good to us—He usually provides each couple with one spender and one saver.

I am truly blessed with a husband who is a wise investor and provider for our family. He doesn't "hoard" in any sense. He takes us on unbelievable vacations, and I've been to places I never dreamed I'd go. But if we hadn't been good stewards over what God blessed us with throughout the years, we would never have had this benefit of enjoying the abundance we now live in.

This brings out another secret to fruitful finances: don't go into marriage when you're young and just starting out with the assumption that you can take elaborate vacations and spend tons of money on luxuries. So many couples purchase all-new furniture, get apartments or housing they can't afford, get themselves way over their heads in debt, and wind up in a mess they can't get out of. This puts unnecessary stress on their relationships. Don't try to live above your means.

I cherish memories from when Chris and I were newlyweds— putting the canned goods in the refrigerator so it wouldn't look as empty, buying our dining set at a yard sale and our first set of "china" that cost all of $19.99, driving an old, beat-up car that would die whenever one of us drove through a mud puddle, and sharing a value meal when we dined out! Over 20 years later, we are driving brand new cars that were purchased FOR us—not by us—living in a home with room to spare. Truly, we lack nothing.

Thank God for small beginnings. They are a BLESSING!

The Apostle Peter gives a few pointers on marriage in his first book: "Husbands, in the same way be considerate as you live with your wives, and treat them with respect as the weaker partner and as heirs with you of the gracious gift of life, so that nothing will hinder your prayers" (1 Peter 3:7). We can take his instructions and apply them to our own marriages, so that nothing hinders our prayers from reaching our Heavenly Father.

In every marriage, there are three areas of relationship. First, husbands must live with their wives according to knowledge. I'm talking specifically about the knowledge found in God's Word about the husband-wife relationship. Secondly, husbands must give their wives honor as unto the weaker vessel; women are not inferior mentally or spiritually—simply physically. Finally, married couples are joint heirs together. The marriage relationship is parallel to the relationship Jesus has with the Church. Just as the members of the Church are joint heirs with Christ, so a wife is a joint heir with her husband.

Our goal as married couples should be to bring to fruition God's will in our spouse's life. Paul explains this explicitly in Ephesians 5:25: "Husbands, love your wives, just as Christ loved the church and gave himself up for her." The Christian husband is responsible for knowing God's will for his wife's life. He should then help her develop into everything God has planned for her. The husband and wife should base their relationship on the knowledge of God's will for both of them. Only then can the windows of heaven be open.

$\star$ $\star$ $\star$ $\star$ $\star$

REASON #12—DISCORD WITH THE BRETHREN

DISCORD COSTS MONEY. THERE IS A LINK between division and strife among Christians and the lack of finances in the Church. Matthew 5:21-24 describes it like this:

> You have heard that it was said to the people long ago, "You shall not murder, and anyone who murders will be subject to judgment." But I tell you that anyone who is angry with a brother or sister will be subject to judgment. Again, anyone who says to a brother or sister, "Raca," is answerable to the court. And anyone who says, "You fool!" will be in danger of the fire of hell.

> Therefore, if you are offering your gift at the altar and there remember that your brother or sister has something against you, leave your gift there in front of the altar. First go and be reconciled to them; then come and offer your gift.

When Christians allow strife among themselves, they render their gifts to God unacceptable. When God rejects your offerings, you automatically exist under a closed heaven. The main reason for this is that strife confuses the lost. It makes it impossible for the world to identify who Jesus really is. If for no other reason, we should avoid it for the sake of unbelievers.

John 13:34-35 says, "A new command I give you: Love one another. As I have loved you, so you must love one another. By this everyone will know that you are my disciples, if you love one another." Jesus knew that division prevents the lost from seeing God's love for them. Among children of God, division and strife work in opposition to God's plan for winning the world.

Our gifts to God need to come to Him purely; and when we can't love our brother, how can we possibly claim to love God? 1 John 4:20 says, "Whoever claims to love God yet hates a brother or sister is a liar. For whoever does not love their brother and sister, whom they have seen, cannot love God, whom they have not seen."

Dissension can be held at bay if you choose not to hold anything against a brother, just as you should not allow your brothers and sisters any reason to hold anything against you. Do everything to love them and walk in unity so that the world may know that Jesus is the Christ, the Son of the Living God. Walk so that the lost may see your love for one another and know also that God loves them. And, Paul advises in Romans 12:18, "If it is possible, as far as it depends on you, live at peace with everyone."

If you are at odds with your brother or sister, or even with an enemy, you are actually rebelling against God. We are instructed in Matthew 5:24, "First go and be reconciled to your brother; then come and offer your gift." God does not even want anything from us unless we first try to make things right between ourselves and anyone who may have ought against us. Only then may we bring our gifts to Him.

If we refuse to reconcile with our brothers and sisters, disobedience or rebellion against God is dealt with very seriously. The Bible puts it like this in 1 Samuel 15:23: "For rebellion is like the sin of divination, and arrogance like the evil of idolatry. Because you have rejected the word of the LORD, he has rejected you as king." Let go of any strife or unforgiveness you may be holding onto. The consequences of discord will reach far deeper than your tested finances. They will determine where you spend eternity.

★ ★ ★ ★ ★

REASON #13—NOT TRUSTING GOD'S MAN

THE CHARISMATIC RENEWAL BROUGHT MANY GOOD THINGS to the Body of Christ. For instance, it has shown the members of the Church to be priests and ministers. However, it also brought with it some bad things. One of the bad things is an attitude of disrespect toward the man of God. This disrespect was not the intention of the Holy Ghost; it was the intervention of the prince of darkness when he tacked on a disrespect for God's appointed leaders to the Body of Christ.

Please do not misunderstand: some so-called leaders do not deserve any respect, for they are nothing more than hirelings. However, the true man of God is to be given double honor, especially if he or she labors in the ministry of the Word of God. This is at the instruction of 1 Timothy 5:17: "The elders who direct the affairs of the church well are worthy of double honor, especially those whose work is preaching and teaching."

Church leaders are gifts. The obedient Christian is to trust and respect His God-appointed leaders, for God "gave gifts unto men," (Ephesians 4:8, KJV). And in Ephesians 4:11-13, we learn that "So Christ himself gave the apostles, the prophets, the evangelists, the pastors and teachers, to equip his people for works of service, so that the body of Christ may be built up until we all reach unity in the faith and in the knowledge of the Son of God and become mature, attaining to the whole measure of the fullness of Christ."

God did not give these five classifications of leaders just for a short season. They were not supposed to become obsolete at the time of the Charismatic renewal. God gave them to the Church for the full age of grace, from the Ascension to the Second Coming. Notice the word, "until" in verse 13. It speaks of the five-fold ministry as being with us until the Church comes into the perfection of "the whole measure of the fullness of Christ."

It is safe to trust the man of God. He will not hinder the priesthood of the believer. He will help it. He does not pose a threat to God's followers. Romans 13:3 proves this: "For rulers hold no terror for those who do right, but for those who do wrong."

The Old Testament further states that you must have a relationship of trust with the prophet (man of God), or you will not prosper. 2 Chronicles 20:20 encourages, "Have faith in the LORD your God and you will be upheld; have faith in his prophets and you will be successful." This Scripture is one of the most neglected I have found, especially when you consider its importance. However, the devil has not overlooked it. He has used it to cripple the Church financially, for he knows full well that, if he can break the confidence between the children of God and their man of God, the prosperity of God will no longer flow into their lives.

How much do you trust your pastor? As much as the widow of Zarephath? 2 Kings 4:1-2 tells her story: "The wife of a man from the company of the prophets cried out to Elisha, 'Your servant my husband is dead, and you know that he revered the LORD. But now his creditor is coming to take my two boys as his slaves.' Elisha replied to her, 'How can I help you? Tell me, what do you have in your house?'

'Your servant has nothing there at all,' she said, 'except a small jar of oil.'"

When the widow goes to Elisha for help with her back-breaking debt, the first thing the prophet asks for is a financial statement. He asks, "What do you have in your house?" Thank God, this widow was able to trust her man of God, for if you read the entire account—through verse seven—you will see that Elisha opened heaven over her life. Her relationship of trust with him set her free from debt, as well as funded her retirement!

We must break the mentality of people who think that "all preachers want is your money."

It should also be noted that no one listens to poor people. If the devil can block you from prospering, he knows he will automatically stop your witness, for he knows no one listens to poor people. Please don't think the devil came up with that idea on his own. He got it from Scripture. God's Word says as much in Ecclesiastes 9:16: "So I said, 'Wisdom is better than strength.' But the poor man's wisdom is despised, and his words are no longer heeded.'"

To be a Christian and live in poverty, with the masses not listening to you, is to live under a closed heaven. Our purpose in living is to win the lost; and if they won't hear us, we have failed.

REASON #14—NOT WORKING

THE TEACHINGS OF THE BOOK OF PROVERBS clearly state the philosophy of the biblical work ethic. One of the most important lessons in that book draws a parallel from one of the smallest creatures in nature. God lays out a plan for success that time has proven to be true. He uses the lowly ant to teach man how to prosper through hard work. In this parallel, the author invites us to visit an ant hill. There, we learn a lesson every person should carefully consider:

"Go to the ant, you sluggard; consider its ways and be wise! It has no commander, no overseer or ruler, yet it stores its provisions in summer and gathers its food at harvest. How long will you lie there, you sluggard? When will you get up from your sleep? A little sleep, a little slumber, a little folding of the hands to rest—and poverty will come on you like a thief and scarcity like an armed man" (Proverbs 6:6-11).

A Christian should be trusted to work unsupervised without robbing his employer of his hourly wage. Good work habits will quickly lead to promotion and increased income. Every Christian should pay special attention to this instruction, for God wants us to be "the head, not the tail" (Deuteronomy 28:13). He wants us to rule, not to be ruled.

God has a "Harvesttime Principle," and Proverbs 6 goes on to show us that the ant is aware of it. Ants realize there is a time to gather. Consequently, they don't starve when an economic depression comes. If the children of God could only get their eyes off the world's predictions of recession and shortage and simply focus on God's promise to the sower, how good it would be for them! Even if a depression comes, the law of sowing and reaping still works. Like the ant, when you learn this lesson, you will never fall victim to recessions and depressions, because "As long as the earth endures, seedtime and harvest, cold and heat, summer and winter, day and night will never cease" (Genesis 8:22).

A person's laziness also guarantees poverty. God goes on to deal harshly with the sin of laziness. He rebukes the sluggard and shows him that the only harvest laziness brings is the harvest of poverty. There is no way to keep poverty away from the lazy person, for the Bible says it comes as an armed robber. It actually says poverty and want will control the lazy man's life. It will be the same with him as it is with the robbery victim. He will be powerless to resist.

The observer in Proverbs 24:30-34 says, "I went past the field of the sluggard, past the vineyard of someone who has no sense; thorns had come up everywhere, the ground was covered with weeds, and the stone wall was in ruins. I applied my heart to what I observed and learned a lesson from what I saw: A little sleep, a little slumber, a little folding of the hands to rest—and poverty will come on you like a thief and scarcity like an armed man."

Non-providers are infidels. The word "infidel" is a translation of a Greek word that literally means "unbeliever." The apostle Timothy said in 1 Timothy 5:8, "Anyone who does not provide for his relatives, and especially for their own household, he has denied the faith and is worse than an unbeliever." Imagine that! A person who refuses to provide for his or her own family becomes worse than an unbeliever before God! Not working places a person under a closed heaven.

That being said, we must cast laziness aside. If you find you have been lazy or have become a non-worker, repent and ask God to help you turn your work habits around. Do what the Word of God tells you in Ecclesiastes 9:10: "Whatever your hand finds to do, do it with all your might."

Perhaps you never learned HOW to be a hard worker. Ephesians 6:5-7 explains exactly how we should perform our service to our employers: "Slaves (employees), obey your earthly masters (employers) with respect and fear, and with sincerity of heart, just as you would obey Christ. Obey them not only to win their favor when their eye is on you, but as slaves of Christ, doing the will of God from your heart. Serve wholeheartedly, as if you were serving the Lord, not people."

Just think of how you would approach your job if Jesus were your employer. Imagine the difference it would make!

★ ★ ★ ★ ★

REASON #15—NO PATIENCE

WAITING IS NOT EASY—FOR ANYONE. HOWEVER, IT does have a purpose. Waiting causes us to hold tight lest what we're waiting for slip away. It also works in us to produce endurance. Perhaps that's why the Bible describes its role in James 1:4: "Let perseverance finish its work so that you may be mature and complete, not lacking anything." Faith and patience go together. Faith is not complete until it is accompanied by patience. The Word of God tells us that, if we do not add patience to our faith, we will never pass the stage of want and need.

Over time, Netta Swift has learned to have patience in her financial situation:

> We have often heard it said that "Patience is a virtue," and that is a true statement; but I HATED IT. I had to have what I wanted—not today, but yesterday. I am one who loves to see it done RIGHT NOW. If I thought of it now, it must manifest now; but I had a rude awakening in my finances.
>
> My husband and I, in our early years of marriage, accumulated a lot of debt though student loans and CREDIT

CARDS, not knowing that, one day, it would catch up with us. For the past several years, we have been trying to recover from it, and in that, my patience wore very thin. Although Rodney is the type to roll with the punches and "Pay our dues," if you will, I said, "God, get us out of this—now!" I felt, since we faithfully paid our tithes and offerings, that "Bam!"—our debt should be gone. But Galatians says that God is not mocked: WHATEVER a man sows, that is what he will reap. We didn't get into debt overnight and, contrary to my hopes, we didn't come out of it overnight.

Instead of focusing on where I wanted to be, as a couple, we began to set short-term goals, and through prayer and being GOOD STEWARDS of what God has allowed us to obtain, we are coming out of debt—quickly. Although we gave out of our need, now we can give out of an easy-flowing fountain and share with the Body of Christ and those in need. We are the lenders and not the borrowers; but my not having patience made this process take longer and hindered our "coming out." Now, all of our credit cards are fully paid off, and we have not put ourselves in a position to get back into debt through credit cards. We are living witnesses of waiting on the Lord to process us. Once we learned to be faithful over the little, God, in our "due season," is making us ruler over much. Praise God for patience. It hurts, but it works.

The New Testament constantly links together faith and patience. The reason is that faith matures only after it faces and passes tests. Your faith must patiently stand until you receive the full manifestation of what you are believing for from God. Only then do you have fully functional faith.

In Romans, the apostle Paul taught this principle when he said, "Therefore, since we have been justified through faith, we have peace with God through our Lord Jesus Christ, through whom we have gained access by faith into this grace in which we now stand. And we boast in the hope of the glory of God. Not only so, but we also glory in our sufferings, because we know that suffering produces perseverance." (Romans 5:1-3).

By closely following Paul's teaching in these verses, you can see the process needed to develop patience: we rejoice in trials and testing. That's a hard statement by itself, for no testing or tribulation is pleasant while it is taking place. This can be seen in his thoughts expressed in verses 3-5: "Not only so, but we also glory in our sufferings, because we know that suffering produces perseverance; perseverance, character; and character, hope. And hope does not put us to shame, because God's love has been poured out into our hearts through the Holy Spirit, who has been given to us."

In this statement, we see the introduction of something new called "hope." Hope speaks of unwavering confidence. When faith matures to the point of being patient, it produces hope—and hope makes us as bold as lions.

Scripture clearly states that you must have patience to receive from God in Hebrews 10:36: "You need to persevere so that when you have done the will of God, you will receive what he has promised." Galatians 6:9 further encourages, "Let us not become weary in doing good, for at the proper time we will reap a harvest if we do not give up" (if we have patience).

Patience is necessary for you to achieve your victory over Satan. Only when you mix your faith with your patience will you have the power to overcome the adversary. This is made clear in Ephesians 6:13-14: "Therefore put on the full armor of God, so that when the day of evil comes, you may be able to stand your ground, and after you have done everything, to stand. Stand firm then, with the belt of truth buckled around your waist, with the breastplate of righteousness in place."

Patience does not happen instantaneously. I wish there were a word I could speak that would give you instant patience, but no such thing exists. You will have to develop your patience in the biblical way. It will have to be the product of the testing of your faith. Remember, without patience, there is no hope of God's best for you. With patience, the windows of heaven open wide.

REASON #16—IMPROPER THINKING

YOU'VE HEARD, "YOU ARE WHAT YOU EAT." Well, "You are what you think" also. The relationship Christians have with God takes place primarily in the mind. (Of course, I speak of the Spirit-dominated mind.) Because of that, the devil puts forth an ongoing effort to influence what goes on in your thinking.

Proverbs 23:6-7 speaks of a person with an evil eye, due to evil thoughts in his mind. These verses warn, "Do not eat the food of a begrudging host, do not crave his delicacies; for he is the kind of person who is always thinking about the cost. "Eat and drink," he says to you, but his heart is not with you."

Thoughts are a creative force. The way you think in your heart will create what you say, and the Bible says you will have whatever you say. Our Lord spoke of the creative force of the mind. Jesus said if we firmly fix our thinking on something, when we speak it, what we say will come to pass. Check out Mark 11:22-24: "'Have faith in God,' Jesus answered. 'Truly I tell you, if anyone says to this mountain, "Go, throw yourself into the sea," and does not doubt in his heart but believes that what they says will happen, it will be done for them. Therefore I tell you, whatever you ask for in prayer, believe that you have received it, and it will be yours.'"

Notice that, while Jesus clearly stated we are to speak to the mountains, He also emphasized that we are to believe firmly and not doubt in our hearts. Once again, we see the English word "heart." Upon examination, we find that the Greek word it represents is better translated "mind." We are to believe and not doubt in our minds.

Your thinking opens or closes heaven. The opposite of this is that, if we don't believe we receive the things we pray for, we won't have them. Our Lord tells us that two mindsets are available to us: we can believe and receive, or we can doubt and do without. The windows of heaven are closed over the person who thinks the wrong way. According to Matthew 21:22, "If you believe, you will receive whatever you ask for in prayer." If you think you will not receive, then you won't.

You can change your thinking, though! You can overcome improper thinking. The apostle Paul gave instructions on how to do this in 2 Corinthians 10:5, when he said, "We demolish arguments and every pretension that sets itself up against the knowledge of God, and we take captive every thought to make it obedient to Christ." The original word "imaginations" can also be translated as "reasoning." Paul said to cast down any reasoning that tries to rise above what you know about God.

For instance, you know God heals. You may experience the symptoms of a sickness. They may manifest themselves in pain or in some inability. Your mind will want to reason from these symptoms that you are sick and may even become sicker. Paul said to cast down that kind of reasoning (imagination). Your body may say, "I am sick," but, as you know, God's Word says, "You are healed." When symptoms come, you must cast down thoughts of sickness because they contradict the knowledge you have about God. His Word says you are already healed.

★　★　★　★　★

REASON #17—
IMPROPER TALKING

THE TONGUE HAS TREMENDOUS POWER. WITH IT, we can do great and wondrous things. We can also do horrible and destructive things. The Apostle James readily recognized its influence. However, he was baffled by the destructive and constructive energy the same tongue was able to produce.

In James 3:8-12, he states, "No human being can tame the tongue. It is a restless evil, full of deadly poison. With the tongue we praise our Lord and Father, and with it we curse human beings, who have been made in God's likeness. Out of the same mouth come praise and cursing. My brothers and sisters, this should not be. Can both fresh water and salt water flow from the same spring? My brothers and sisters, can a fig tree bear olives, or a grapevine bear figs? Neither can a salt spring produce fresh water." The apostle's frustration was evident as he pondered the possibility of both bitter and sweet water coming forth from the same fountain. He wondered how the same member of the body that blesses God could also curse a man. James went on to say that the destructive force of the tongue can ignite the entire system of darkness.

James 3:5-6 states, "Likewise, the tongue is a small part of the body, but it makes great boasts. Consider what a great forest is set on fire by a small spark. The tongue also is a fire, a world of evil among the parts of the body. It corrupts the whole body, sets the whole course of one's life on fire, and is itself set on fire by hell." We can better understand the phrase "sets the whole course of one's life on fire" if we paraphrase it as follows: "The tongue re-ignites the old nature and sets it back on its course of destruction."

We can further see the two extreme abilities of the tongue in Proverbs 18:21: "The tongue has the power of life and death, and those who love it will eat its fruit." Your tongue can be a life-giver or a life-taker. It all depends on how you choose to use it.

Let's look at the positive aspects of the tongue. If you use it correctly, it can become the source of your life. By your tongue, you can bring forth abundance, according to Proverbs 18:20: "From the fruit of their mouth a person's stomach is filled; with the harvest of their lips they are satisfied." Three words stand out in this verse: "satisfied," "harvest," and "filled." What you speak can satisfy your appetite. The words of your lips can cause you to increase in substance. What your words produce can fill you with good things.

Look further at Proverbs 15:4: "The soothing tongue is a tree of life, but a perverse tongue crushes the spirit." Your words can become a tree of supply for the needs and desires of your life, or your words can cause death. God's Word literally says that wrong speaking punctures the spirit. Again, Proverbs 12:18 asserts, "The words of the reckless pierce like swords, but the tongue of the wise brings healing."

The person who speaks truth establishes himself throughout eternity. But the same tongue that has the potential to establish a person forever also has the ability to send him into oblivion, according to Proverbs 12:19: "Truthful lips endure forever, but a lying tongue lasts only a moment."

How accurate the evaluation of James is! The tongue that can bring life can also inflict a mortal wound. The tongue that can be the balm of health can also be the sword of piercing. The tongue that can tie you to eternal life can also doom you to destruction.

Now, let's look at how the tongue can open and close the windows of heaven. An important Old Testament account that the Church doesn't seem to understand clarifies a perfect illustration of how we should talk if we want to keep heaven open.

In 2 Kings 4:8-27, we find the story of a barren woman who conceives and delivers a son after the man of God prays for her. The boy grows up, and one day, as he is working in the field with his father, he becomes sick. We know from verses 20 and 32 that the child dies. The mother goes to a nearby city to speak to Elisha. When the husband asks why she is going to see the man of God, her answer was a perfect application of proper speaking. She said, "It shall be well."

When Elisha sees her coming, he sends his servant to inquire of her if all is well. He asks about her husband and son—notice how she answers his question. She replies, "All is well." At this point, most of us would have begun to cry and wail, "He is dead!" Not so with this woman. When Elisha comes to her home, he ministers life to her child. This woman did not allow the words of death to come out of her mouth. She only spoke life; and in doing so, she was able to hold off the death angel just long enough for the prophet to arrive and raise her son from the dead.

The way you talk can determine whether or not the windows of heaven stay open. If you speak words of sickness, pain, and disease while you are believing for healing, your words will swing the balance of power in favor of sickness. However, if you speak words of health, the balance of power will swing toward your healing.

Agreement has tremendous power. You can agree with sickness or with health. You can agree with poverty or prosperity. It's up to you. If your words agree with the undesirable circumstances that are trying to overtake you, then they will surely happen. When you speak words of agreement with adverse symptoms, you strengthen their hold on your life. If your words agree with the promises of Jesus, you strengthen the hold of the promises on your life.

REASON #18—UNPAID VOWS

THE WORD "VOW" IS NOT COMMONLY USED in modern-day Christianity. However, it does appear over 90 times in the Bible. The normally used word for vow is "pledge." A pledge is a promise to give or do something in the future. Most Christians have made a pledge or, at the very least, they've heard someone use the word.

Between the 1950s and mid-1980s, the Church in North America made a tremendous number of pledges. We called this form of giving "faith-promise giving." The way faith-promise giving worked was that the giver would pledge to give a certain amount, although many times, he did not have the money at the time to pay the pledge. The person would then pay his pledge by giving an amount weekly or monthly.

When, in the early 1980s, Christian television in America had begun to really grow, something went wrong. People began to wildly pledge large sums of money. The amounts of these promises were astounding. But there was a problem: Few people were faithful in paying what they had pledged.

Throughout the years, many Christians have made pledges they have not kept. God's Word is clear about His attitude toward vowing and not paying: He doesn't like it! Ecclesiastes 5:4-5 states, "When you make a vow to God, do not delay in fulfilling it. He has no pleasure in fools; fulfill your vow. It is better not to vow than to make a vow and not fulfill it." Those who vow and do not pay are fools, and He has no pleasure in them.

God expects payment of what a person vows, and it is sin to vow and not pay. "If you make a vow to the LORD your God, do not be slow to pay it, for the LORD your God will certainly demand it of you and you will be guilty of sin. But if you refrain from making a vow, you will not be guilty. Whatever your lips utter you must be sure to do, because you made your vow freely to the LORD your God with your own mouth" (Deuteronomy 23:21-23).

When we study the subject of vows, it becomes evident from Scripture that God is in favor of His children making vows. The Bible actually tells us that, when we make proper vows, God quickly moves into action. The case of Hannah's vow shows God's fast response in answering her prayer. In I Samuel, Hannah vowed to give God her son if He would only give her one to give Him.

I Samuel 1:11 says, "[Hannah] made a vow, saying, 'LORD Almighty, if you will only look upon your servant's misery and remember me, and not forget your servant but give her a son, then I will give him to the LORD for all the days of his life, and no razor will ever be used on his head.'"

The answer to Hannah's prayer came in just a few days when she and her husband returned home. The biblical account of 1 Samuel 1:19 says, "Early the next morning they arose and worshiped before the LORD and then went back to their home at Ramah. Elkanah made love to Hannah, and the LORD remembered her."

If you have any unpaid vows, you can rectify them. Two Scriptures have to do with correcting unpaid vows. Leviticus discusses vows of specific amounts and specific things. When you read Leviticus 27:13—"If the owner wishes to redeem the animal, a fifth must be added to its value"—you will find a statement about the promise of a beast. If the person who promised the beast changes his mind and does not want to give it, he is to add 20 percent to its value and give God the money.

This verse means that a 20 percent penalty is due on unfulfilled vows. This form of settling unpaid vows would be difficult to apply in this present dispensation of grace, for most Christians don't give animals to God. Because our vows are usually in the form of money, the solution of a 20 percent penalty seems to be out of the question. If a person cannot pay the original amount of money he promised, it is doubtful he would be able to pay 20 percent more.

If you have unpaid pledges or vows, you need to correct them. If you have the money to pay your pledge, you need to pay what you promised. This is the ideal solution. However, if you do not have the money to pay the pledges, you need to do the following. First of all, go to God and ask Him to forgive you. Then, ask Him to reveal an amount of money you can pay toward your pledges. If you have made pledges to more than one ministry, equally divide that amount among the ministries. Send each ministry part and ask to be released from the remaining balance of your promise.

The problem of unpaid vows may seem great, but our God is even greater. Make things right, and whatever you do, don't stop pledging. Just start paying every faith promise you make, and you will open the windows of heaven over your life.

★ ★ ★ ★ ★

REASON #19—UNJUST STEWARDSHIP

WE ARE THE PURCHASED PROPERTY OF GOD. As hard as it is to get this concept into our thinking, we must realize that Christians are not independent operators. 1 Corinthians 6:19-20 (KJV) says, "Know ye not that…ye are not your own? For ye are bought with a price." From the day we are saved, everything we are and everything we have becomes the Lord's. This includes our earning power. Even though many Christians do not know this truth, Scripture is clear about it. God says our very ability to earn money comes directly from Him.

Deuteronomy 8:17-19 says, "You may say to yourself, 'My power and the strength of my hands have produced this wealth for me.' But remember the LORD your God, for it is he who gives you the ability to produce wealth, and so confirms his covenant, which he swore to your forefathers, as it is today. If you ever forget the LORD your God and follow other gods and worship and bow down to them, I testify against you today that you will surely be destroyed."

From these verses, we can see that our ability to obtain wealth doesn't come from within ourselves. God says our earning power comes from Him. Notice that this truth does not end here. The Scripture goes on to say that God has a claim on the wealth He empowers us to get. It is for the specific purpose of establishing the covenant.

God has given you the power to get wealth so that you can be His faithful steward. You must now make a decision: is the money you earn yours—to fund your lifestyle—or does it belong to God to fund His end-time harvest?

The Apostle Paul was careful to emphasize that stewards have the right to enjoy a generous portion of their labor. In 1 Corinthians 9:8-10, he asks, "Do I say this merely on human authority? Doesn't the Law say the same thing? For it is written in the Law of Moses: "Do not muzzle an ox while it is treading out the grain." Is it about oxen that God is concerned? Surely he says this for us, doesn't he? Yes, this was written for us, because whoever plows and threshes should be able to do so in the hope of sharing in the harvest."

If you operate as a faithful steward, the Lord will take proper care of you. Jesus firmly established this truth when He spoke of the reward his faithful servants will receive in Matthew 25:20-21: "The man who had received five bags of gold brought the other five. 'Master,' he said, 'you entrusted me with five bags of gold. See, I have gained five more.' His master replied, 'Well done, good and faithful servant! You have been faithful with a few things; I will put you in charge of many things. Come and share your master's happiness!'"

God improved this servant's lifestyle when He saw the quality of his stewardship. Most Christians today do not operate this way. They are trying to establish a good lifestyle so they can give into the gospel. This way sounds good, but it is not according to biblical pattern. Jesus is not looking for people who will fund the gospel out of their possessions; instead, He wants to develop faithful stewards who will become managers of His assets. The better these stewards manage His affairs, the better quality of life He will provide for them.

It's amazing that seemingly intelligent people can seriously believe that anything on planet Earth is their own, exclusive property.

It would seem that created beings on a created planet would have to belong to God, who created them.

Please hear God's opinion of this matter. He says throughout the Bible that everything belongs to Him. He says that all the earth and its fullness are His personal possession:

Psalm 24:1: "The earth is the Lord's, and everything in it, the world, and all who live in it."

Psalm 50:10-12: "For every animal of the forest is mine, and the cattle on a thousand hills. I know every bird in the mountains, and the insects in the field are mine. If I were hungry I would not tell you, for the world is mine, and all that is in it."

Haggai 2:8: "'The silver is mine and the gold is mine,' declares the LORD Almighty."

God says everything is His. Surely, the informed child of God must conclude that he or she is a steward and not a proprietor. God has given you only temporary oversight of the few possessions you control.

There is a secret that will forever release you from having a problem when God asks you to give. You must understand that everything you control belongs to God. If you can realize this fact, you can benefit from it too. The secret is this: simply give everything you have and everything you ever will have to God. From the day you do, you will no longer be giving that which is yours—you will merely be redistributing that which is God's.

If unjust stewardship has closed the windows of heaven over your life, here is what you should do. Rise up and begin to tithe and give proper offerings. Prove to God that you are concerned about His business, and that you want Him to reinstate your stewardship. When God sees that are serious about the Kingdom, surely He will return your stewardship to you.

★　★　★　★　★

REASON #20—NOT DISCERNING THE BODY

A LARGE AMOUNT OF OUR FINANCES ARE TAKEN up by food purchases. With today's fast-paced society, it is so easy to fall into the "fast food trap." As mentioned in 1 Corinthians 11:29 (KJV), "He...eateth and drinketh damnation to himself, not discerning the Lord's body." As a result, we can plan on spending even more money on doctors' bills trying to reverse the damage we cause in our bodies! Dr. Malcolm Hill offers these words of wisdom concerning one's health:

> There are many ways we can close the windows of heaven by not taking care of the body, but I will focus on the final result of not being a good steward with the body—death. There have been many Christians who had missions from God but were not able to complete them because they did not take care of their physical bodies. Once death comes upon your physical body, your mission stops, and the windows of heaven close in your life.

You may be called to be a preacher, teacher, intercessor, apostle, bishop, etc., but if you do not take care of your physical body, you may not get to enjoy the wholeness of God. You may end up battling with a disease. It is all too common in today's society that we hear about a man of God battling with cancer, diabetes, a stroke or heart attack, arthritis, high blood pressure and high blood cholesterol.

This happens because many ministers live spiritually, yet forget to take care of their physical bodies. So, take care of your body by eating godly foods (fruits, vegetables, whole grains, raw nuts and seeds, water) and exercising on a regular basis. When you do this, you will live a normal lifespan (120 yrs.) as God intended and get to enjoy all the treats that the windows of heaven have to offer you.

Many times, traditional interpretations obscure the simplest truths in God's Word. One reason they do is that the Body of Christ is out of balance in the areas of teaching and preaching. We have become a people who hear much preaching but far too little teaching. I'm not saying preaching is not important—I'm simply saying that Christians need more teaching. One of the main differences between preaching and teaching is that teaching involves the context of the Scriptures, while preaching usually involves the emotional response of the listeners more than context.

Because of a lack of teaching on the subject, we don't have a proper understanding of the Body of Christ. Much modern preaching has focused its attention primarily on the flesh-and-blood body of Jesus. It's necessary for us to know of the agony He bore in His physical body in order to understand properly the price He paid for our everlasting life. However, when we hear preaching only about Christ's physical body, it's easy to lose sight of His corporate body— the Body of Christ—that walks the earth today. We, the saints of God, make up His Church.

1 Corinthians 12:27 assures us in this way: "Now you are the Body of Christ, and each one of you is a part of it." Every person who is

born again is a part of the Body of Christ, because he has Jesus living inside him. We know this based on Colossians 1:27: "To them God has chosen to make known among the Gentiles the glorious riches of this mystery, which is Christ in you, the hope of glory."

Since Jesus is in you, you are the Body of Christ. Scripture, as a whole, goes beyond the concept of each of us individually being the bodies of Christ—it groups us together as individual parts that collectively become one great body, His Body on earth as can be seen in 1 Corinthians 12:12-14: "Just as a body, though one, has many parts, but all its many parts form one body, so it is with Christ. For we were all baptized by one Spirit so as to form one body—whether Jews or Gentiles, slave or free—and we were all given the one Spirit to drink. 14 Even so the body is not made up of one part but of many."

Each time we take communion, it is possible that we close heaven over our lives. We do this if we don't discern our Lord's Body.

> For I received from the Lord what I also passed on to you: The Lord Jesus, on the night he was betrayed, took bread, and when he had given thanks, he broke it and said, "This is my body, which is for you; do this in remembrance of me." In the same way, after supper he took the cup, saying, "This cup is the new covenant in my blood; do this, whenever you drink it, in remembrance of me." For whenever you eat this bread and drink this cup, you proclaim the Lord's death until he comes.

> So then, whoever eats the bread or drinks the cup of the Lord in an unworthy manner will be guilty of sinning against the body and blood of the Lord. Everyone ought to examine themselves before they eat of the bread and drink from the cup. For those who eat and drink without discerning the body of Christ eat and drink judgment on themselves. That is why many among you are weak and sick, and a number of you have fallen asleep (1 Corinthians 11:23-30).

This Scripture clearly says that not discerning the Body of Christ brings big problems upon the church. Paul said it causes weakness, sickness, and death. Surely, these words speak of a closed heaven. The word "discerning" is the translation of a Greek word that means "recognizing and giving proper place to a thing." Here, the word literally means that we are to give preferential treatment to the Body of Christ.

At first glance, you may think the Word of God is speaking primarily of discerning the flesh-and-blood body of Jesus. However, after a deeper study of the subject, we find it is speaking of His corporate Body, the Church. We need to take into account 1 Corinthians 10:15-17, where Paul says, "I speak to sensible people; judge for yourselves what I say. Is not the cup of thanksgiving for which we give thanks a participation in the blood of Christ? And is not the bread that we break a participation in the body of Christ? Because there is one loaf, we, who are many, are one body, for we all partake of the one loaf." He specifically recognizes the Body of Christ as the Church. Paul says it is wise to understand that we are the bread of the communion, and we all take a part in that one bread (loaf), which is the Church.

We need to discern properly the Lord's Body. Please stop now and look at the Christian who is nearest you. Now, say out loud, "This person (say the person's name) is part of the Body of Christ." Now, think of your pastor. He is part of the Body of Christ. Every born-again member of your church is a part of the Body of Christ. Think of some distant land where Christians are persecuted, and realize those unknown saints are a part of the Body of Christ, as well.

Open your eyes with new understanding. Each time you see a brother or sister in Christ, force yourself to look at him or her in a new way. No longer see a Methodist, Baptist, or just a member of some church. From this day on, look upon each believer as the Church, the Body of Christ.

If you can begin to look at all Christians with this new viewpoint, you will find that your whole attitude toward the brethren will change. The way you treat fellow Christians will change. With this new outlook, heaven will open!

REASON #21—LOVING MONEY

TRANSLATORS COULD PROBABLY HAVE BETTER INTER-PRETED THE following verse: "The love of money is a root of all kinds of evil" (1 Timothy 6:10). A constant chain of actions and reactions takes place in the life of a person who loves money. He may not notice this activity at first, but in time, money will totally dominate his life. Many times, the love of money will manifest itself in the form of materialism.

Materialism is a strong force. People have rightly called it "The God of the 20th Century." Most people spend the major part of each day in pursuit of material possessions. Please don't think from this statement that God is against your having nice things. Jesus Himself said that your Heavenly Father knows you need material things in Matthew 6:32: "For the pagans run after all these things, and your heavenly Father knows that you need them." It is obvious from God's Word that material things are not outside His will for His children. The problem with materialism is that it takes the collection of things out of its proper place.

To the person caught in the web of materialism, gathering things becomes more important than anything else. It eventually becomes more important than even God Himself.

Jesus put material possessions in their proper perspective in Matthew 6:33—He said, "But seek first his kingdom and his righteousness, and all these things will be given to you as well." And, when you put God first, He can take pleasure in your prosperity as stated in Psalm 35:27: "May those who delight in my vindication shout for joy and gladness; may they always say, 'The LORD be exalted, who delights in the well-being of his servant.'"

However, if you put things first, don't expect anything to go right in the spirit world.

Materialism is by no means at the root of the problem. It is not a cause; rather, it's an effect of something much deeper that's taking place inside a person. Materialism is the outward manifestation of an inward greed. Greed is a horrible thing. It is pure evil. Greed has an appetite nothing can satisfy. God brands a man a "fool" for having greed. It's the force that drives the dying billionaire as he reaches out for just one more dollar. It's the force that drove the rich farmer in Luke 12 to tear down his barns and build larger ones.

> And he told them this parable: "The ground of a certain rich man yielded an abundant harvest. He thought to himself, 'What shall I do? I have no place to store my crops.'

> "Then he said, 'This is what I'll do. I will tear down my barns and build bigger ones, and there I will store my surplus grain. And I'll say to myself, "You have plenty of grain laid up for many years. Take life easy; eat, drink and be merry."'

> "But God said to him, 'You fool! This very night your life will be demanded from you. Then who will get what you have prepared for yourself?'

"This is how it will be with whoever stores up things for themselves but is not rich toward God." (Luke 12:16-21).

Greed will stop at nothing to satisfy its hunger. It is truly impossible to please.

Now, we come to the root cause of materialism and greed. It is idolatry. I'm not speaking of the worship of things, but of gathering things for the worship of *self*. Self-love can replace the love of God in a person's life. When our basic drive is no longer the desire to worship God, we quickly and forcefully turn to self-worship. God's Word speaks clearly against any worship in which we don't totally focus on Him. The Ten Commandments open and close with decrees against it. The first commands, "Thou shalt have no other gods before me," (Exodus 20:3, KJV). Plainly, self-worship is wrong. The last commandment says, "Thou shall not covet...any thing that is thy neighbor's" (Exodus 20:17, KJV). This commandment is also against self-worship, for covetousness is the desire to present things to ourselves as a form of worship.

How powerful the love of money is! 1 Timothy 6:9 (KJV) describes it: "But they that will be rich fall into temptation and a snare, and into many foolish and hurtful lusts, which drown men in destruction and perdition." This tells us the awful results that come to those who love money. The phrase "they that will be rich" actually means, "they that purpose to become rich." It speaks of having an affectionate desire for riches. The Bible tells us that people whose purpose in life is to gain wealth will fall into temptation—they will begin to follow many foolish lusts. In verse 10, Paul goes on to say, "For the love of money is the root of all evil: which while some coveted after, they have erred from the faith, and pierced themselves through with many sorrows." Clearly, the person who allows himself to love money has a real problem. It is impossible for him to live under an open heaven.

There's nothing wrong with having money, as long as money doesn't have you. If you find yourself caught in the trap of loving money, immediately confess your sin to God. Break the hold that money has had over you by making bold plans to start giving some of it away.

Zacchaeus remedied his love of money by giving, and Jesus bore witness to the victory he won. Luke 19:8-9 tells us that "Zacchaeus stood up and said to the Lord, 'Look, Lord! Here and now I give half of my possessions to the poor, and if I have cheated anybody out of anything, I will pay back four times the amount.' Jesus said to him, 'Today salvation has come to this house, because this man, too, is a son of Abraham.'"

Begin to expose yourself to opportunities to give. Involve yourself in specific projects of generosity. Find a family less fortunate than you and start helping them with their financial burdens. Any or all of these suggestions should help you shake off the love of money and open the window of blessing. Remember, "It is more blessed to give than to receive," (Acts 20:35).

REASON #22—IMPROPER UPBRINGING

THE WAY WE ARE RAISED HAS DEFINITE consequences on our adult life. Scott Combs explains to us in his personal testimony how this was the case in his life:

My upbringing was not unlike hundreds of other people across the USA. I was told, "Get a good job, buy a house, two cars, and have a credit card or two. If there is any money left over, start a savings account." There wasn't much talk of the future, and at retirement, you were just to do the best you could.

With this mindset, I found myself divorced, with two car payments, a mortgage, $13,000 dollars in credit card debt, no savings or retirement, and a hefty child support payment each month. I was facing all of this at the age of just 35.

However, a new century brought with it a new mindset for me. Paul tells us in Romans 12:2 to "Be transformed by the renewing of your mind." This word became a revelation to me. Armed with this new philosophy and a new marriage, things began to turn around.

With a new commitment to God and lots of hard work, we now have zero credit card debt, a mortgage, only one car payment, and a modest retirement and savings account. Our credit score is outstanding, and this was accomplished in just six years. Praise God for second chances!

We still have a way to go before we reach our goals of becoming debt-free, but with God's help, we know without a shadow of doubt that we will reach our goal.

Proverbs 22:6 says, "Start children off on the way they should go, and even when they are old they will not turn from it." This verse is speaking primarily of financial training. Traditionally, it's been quoted as if its message were complete as it appears in verse 6 alone. The truth of the matter is that the thought is incomplete without the addition of verse 7. Only when we add verse seven does its true meaning come forth. Let's look at both verses together: "Start children off on the way they should go, and even when they are old they will not turn from it. The rich rule over the poor, and the borrower is slave to the lender."

How different the meaning becomes when we see it in its full context. It's no longer a catch-all, child-raising verse, but instead a strict warning to parents. It tells them two things that will happen if they bring up their children in a household of debt: First, their children will not depart from that lifestyle when they became older; and second, they are likely to live their lives as servants of the rich.

Are you training your children to live in debt? It's hard to imagine that you might actually be training your children to be debtors. However, it's a real possibility, especially when you realize just how much exposure to debt your children have. The truth is that we actually surround them with it.

Let me run down a small list of the debt-oriented things to which we expose our children each day...

- They live in houses with thirty-year mortgages.

- They wear clothes purchased with credit cards.
- Those same clothes are washed in washing machines purchased on monthly payment plans.
- They study from mortgaged encyclopedias.
- They watch mortgaged televisions.
- They sleep on mortgaged beds.

They are born into families up to their eyeballs in debt. They live eighteen to twenty-five years in this debt-ridden environment; and when they are old enough to drive, we usually co-sign a bank loan for them to purchase their first automobile. By doing so, we launch them into their own ocean of debt, never to be free again.

As the proverb says, parents have trained their children to be in debt. From their earliest childhood years, they have seen nothing but debt. Then, as adults, they become prisoners of debt.

Prisoners of debt face a gloomy future. A pleasant saying about those who live under an open heaven goes like this: "Your future looks bright." The borrower usually cannot say these words about himself because only his past looks bright. The road ahead looks dark and uneventful, because he has committed a large part of his future to paying for his past enjoyments. This situation is most surely not God's best!

However, there is good news! You can overcome this debt-training. If you are a prisoner of debt, you must do three things before you can be free. First, pray to God to break the spirit of debt over your life. Then, you must stop buying on credit. Chop up the credit cards. Third, you must start on a good get-out-of-debt plan immediately. Make the decision now that the generational curse of financial bondage ends with you.

REASON #23—NOT HEARING THE POOR

G OD TELLS US IN MATTHEW 25:40, "WHATEVER you did for one of the least of these brothers and sisters of mine, you did for me." That means that, when we feed the hungry, it is as if we are feeding Him!

Our church is blessed to have people with a burning desire to be conduits of God's blessing. They have dedicated themselves to meeting the needs of others. Here is a personal account from minister Mira Green:

> God has allowed us to be there for so many people, but one lady comes to mind that we are presently helping. She came by the church one day in need of food assistance. She had just lost her job because her company closed, and she didn't have enough money left for bills and food. We assisted her with the food, prayed with her, and continued to help with her needs.

After a few months, she ended up in jail and had to serve several months because of a domestic dispute. Two of her children were taken away from her, and another one lived with a relative; but God had it all set up because while she was in jail, someone started talking to her about Jesus.

When she was released from jail, she came back to us, gave her life to the Lord, and is now a member of Living Faith. She's ready to walk into the abundant life that God has in store for her. We are now helping her find a job and, eventually, when she gets back on her feet, get her children back. God is so good.

This is just one of many situations that we try to help people through.

According to Proverbs 21:13, "Whoever shuts their ears to the cry of the poor will also cry out and not be answered." If you don't have a sympathetic ear for the poor, you are guaranteed to eventually find yourself in trouble. Notice how emphatically that verse puts it. If you don't hear the cry of the poor, you will cry one day, but no one will hear you. Not hearing the poor will bring you under a closed heaven.

A better choice is to lend to the Lord. Most people don't realize the strong connection between God and the poor of this world. When you have compassion on the poor by giving them money, food, or supply, your gift to them becomes a loan to God. It is a loan that God Himself promises to repay in Proverbs 19:17: "Whoever is kind to the poor lends to the Lord, and he will reward them for what they have done."

Jesus directed much of His ministry to the poor. When He described His anointing, He included them: "The Spirit of the Lord is on me, because he has anointed me to preach good news to the poor. He has sent me to proclaim freedom for the prisoners and recovery of sight for the blind, to set the oppressed free." (Luke 4:18).

Let's look at the reason God requires us to minister to the poor. Isaiah 51:1 says, "Listen to me, you who pursue righteousness and who seek the LORD: Look to the rock from which you were cut and to the quarry from which you were hewn."

Through the prophet Isaiah, God instructs us to remember the miserable state of moral and spiritual poverty we were in before He saved us. It's good for us to remember that we were in the deepest possible form of poverty—we were bankrupt in the court of God's righteous judgment. When we cried out from our point of need, God generously gave us salvation!

God's Word is clear about the poor: He expects more from His children than a hearty, "God bless you!" It will take your personal involvement in helping the poor solve their problems to satisfy God's expectation of you. You cannot simply pass over them with a prayer.

Please hear what the Apostle James says on this subject: "What good is it, my brothers and sisters, if someone claims to have faith but has no deeds? Can such faith save them? Suppose a brother or a sister is without clothes and daily food. If one of you says to them, "Go in peace; keep warm and well fed," but does nothing about their physical needs, what good is it? In the same way, faith by itself, if it is not accompanied by action, is dead" (James 2:14-17).

James says real faith constantly proves itself by performing good works. Notice that the illustration James uses to show good works isn't leaving gospel tracts in public restrooms or serving on the cleanup committee at church. Instead, he chooses feeding the hungry and clothing the naked as validating actions of faith.

It's also wise to bless and have compassion on the poor. God makes special promises to those who consider the poor in Psalm 41:1-2: "Blessed are those who have regard for the weak; the Lord delivers them in times of trouble. The Lord protects and preserves them—they are counted among the blessed in the land—he does not give them over to the desire of their foes."

God will look at your actions toward the poor in one of two ways. Proverbs 14:31 tells us what they are: "Whoever oppresses the poor shows contempt for their Maker, but whoever is kind to the needy honors God." Do your actions insult or honor?

We must open our ears to the poor. We must get busy. Feed the hungry, clothe the naked, and assist the down-and-out. The Word of God assures us that God looks upon this kind of activity with great pleasure.

REASON #24—HIDDEN SIN

PSALM 66:18 (KJV) PRONOUNCES, "IF I REGARD iniquity in my heart, the Lord will not hear me." The psalmist strategically chose the word "iniquity," which literally means "that which comes to nothing." We use this word in relation to idols, wickedness, vanity, and worthless things. When I saw how broad the definition was, I wondered if I had chosen the right verse for this chapter. However, the longer I looked at it, the more convinced I became that it was the perfect verse. The word iniquity covers *every* hidden sin of which a person might possibly be guilty.

Carefully read Ephesians 4:17—6:18 in The Living Bible:

> Let me say this, then, speaking for the Lord: Live no longer as So I tell you this, and insist on it in the Lord, that you must no longer live as the Gentiles do, in the futility of their thinking. They are darkened in their understanding and separated from the life of God because of the ignorance that is in them due to the hardening of their hearts. Having lost all sensitivity, they have given themselves over to sensuality

so as to indulge in every kind of impurity, and they are full of greed.

That, however, is not the way of life you learned when you heard about Christ and were taught in him in accordance with the truth that is in Jesus. You were taught, with regard to your former way of life, to put off your old self, which is being corrupted by its deceitful desires; to be made new in the attitude of your minds; and to put on the new self, created to be like God in true righteousness and holiness.

Therefore each of you must put off falsehood and speak truthfully to your neighbor, for we are all members of one body. "In your anger do not sin": Do not let the sun go down while you are still angry, and do not give the devil a foothold. Anyone who has been stealing must steal no longer, but must work, doing something useful with their own hands, that they may have something to share with those in need.

Do not let any unwholesome talk come out of your mouths, but only what is helpful for building others up according to their needs, that it may benefit those who listen. And do not grieve the Holy Spirit of God, with whom you were sealed for the day of redemption. Get rid of all bitterness, rage and anger, brawling and slander, along with every form of malice. Be kind and compassionate to one another, forgiving each other, just as in Christ God forgave you. Follow God's example, therefore, as dearly loved children and walk in the way of love, just as Christ loved us and gave himself up for us as a fragrant offering and sacrifice to God.

But among you there must not be even a hint of sexual immorality, or of any kind of impurity, or of greed, because these are improper for God's holy people. Nor should there be obscenity, foolish talk or coarse joking, which are out of place, but rather thanksgiving. For of this you can be sure: No immoral, impure or greedy person—such a person is an idolater—has any inheritance in the kingdom of Christ and of God. Let no one deceive you with empty words, for because of such things God's wrath comes on those who are disobedient. Therefore do not be partners with them.

For you were once darkness, but now you are light in the Lord. Live as children of light (for the fruit of the light consists in all goodness, righteousness and truth) and find out what pleases the Lord. Have nothing to do with the fruitless deeds of darkness, but rather expose them. It is shameful even to mention what the disobedient do in secret. But everything exposed by the light becomes visible—and everything that is illuminated becomes a light. This is why it is said:

> "Wake up, sleeper,
>   rise from the dead,
>   and Christ will shine on you."

Be very careful, then, how you live—not as unwise but as wise, making the most of every opportunity, because the days are evil. Therefore do not be foolish, but understand what the Lord's will is. Do not get drunk on wine, which leads to debauchery. Instead, be filled with the Spirit, speaking to one another with psalms, hymns, and songs from the Spirit. Sing and make music from your heart to the Lord, always giving thanks to God the Father for everything, in the name of our Lord Jesus Christ.

Submit to one another out of reverence for Christ. Wives, submit yourselves to your own husbands as you do to the Lord. For the husband is the head of the wife as Christ is the head of the church, his body, of which he is the Savior. Now as the church submits to Christ, so also wives should submit to their husbands in everything.

Husbands, love your wives, just as Christ loved the church and gave himself up for her to make her holy, cleansing[c] her by the washing with water through the word, and to present her to himself as a radiant church, without stain or wrinkle or any other blemish, but holy and blameless. In this same way, husbands ought to love their wives as their own bodies. He who loves his wife loves himself. After all, no one ever hated their own body, but they feed and care for their body, just as Christ does the church— for we are members of his body. "For this reason a man will leave his father and mother and be united to his wife, and the two will become one flesh." This is a profound mystery—but I am talking about Christ and the church. However, each one of you also must love his wife as he loves himself, and the wife must respect her husband.

Children, obey your parents in the Lord, for this is right. "Honor your father and mother"—which is the first commandment with a promise—"so that it may go well with you and that you may enjoy long life on the earth." Fathers, do not exasperate your children; instead, bring them up in the training and instruction of the Lord.

Slaves, obey your earthly masters with respect and fear, and with sincerity of heart, just as you would obey Christ. Obey them not only to win their favor when their eye is on you, but as slaves of Christ, doing the will of God from your heart. Serve wholeheartedly, as if you were serving the Lord, not people, because you know that the Lord will reward each one for whatever good they do, whether they are slave or free.

And masters, treat your slaves in the same way. Do not threaten them, since you know that he who is both their Master and yours is in heaven, and there is no favoritism with him.

Finally, be strong in the Lord and in his mighty power. Put on the full armor of God, so that you can take your stand against the devil's schemes. For our struggle is not against flesh and blood, but against the rulers, against the authorities, against the powers of this dark world and against the spiritual forces of evil in the heavenly realms. Therefore put on the full armor of God, so that when the day of evil comes, you may be able to stand your ground, and after you have done everything, to stand. Stand firm then, with the belt of truth buckled around your waist, with the breastplate of righteousness in place, and with your feet fitted with the readiness that comes from the gospel of peace. In addition to all this, take up the shield of faith, with which you can extinguish all the flaming arrows of the evil one. Take the helmet of salvation and the sword of the Spirit, which is the word of God.

And pray in the Spirit on all occasions with all kinds of prayers and requests. With this in mind, be alert and always keep on praying for all the Lord's people.

I am believing that this special section of the Word of God has done its work and revealed any sin that you might have hidden in your heart. If it has, quickly confess it to God and repent of it. You must also forsake it if you hope to live under God's open heaven, for God says in Proverbs 28:13, "Whoever conceals their sins does not prosper, but the one who confesses and renounces them finds mercy."

Don't be afraid of confessing your sins. As soon as you confess them, you render them powerless over you. Acts 3:19 says, "Repent, then, and turn to God, so that your sins may be wiped out." The blood of Jesus literally blots out our sins.

Remember, God will not hear you if you have hidden sin in your heart. However, when you identify it, confess it, repent of it, and forsake it, sin will lose its power and heaven will open over you.

REASON #25—TRADITION

IN HIS GOSPEL, MATTHEW ACCUSES, "YOU NULLIFY the word of God for the sake of your tradition" (15:6). Religious tradition falls into two basic categories: one pertains to ceremonies, and the other has to do with interpretation. From this point on in our study, we'll refer to them as "ceremonial traditions" and "traditional interpretations."

The devil enjoys it when the ceremonial traditions of the church divide it. We don't need to stick to the traditions of the church to move the hand of God. Someone can receive a physical healing in a fancy building or in a simple one; God can bless people in a cathedral just as easily as in an auditorium.

However, traditional interpretations are the real enemies of the Word of God. Every denomination has done its part to contribute to the problem. Each time men adjust Scripture to fit their doctrines, they add to the ever-growing list of erroneous interpretations.

Although these misinterpretations are common and widely accepted, they must be removed, or they will cause the Word of God to render no effect in your life. It's one thing to not know about these traditional interpretations; but when you are walking in tradition knowingly and doing nothing about it, it becomes sin. James 4:17 (KJV) says so: "To him that knoweth to do good, and doeth it not, to him it is sin."

This type of behavior becomes even more serious when it involves knowing the truth of God's Word and not acting on it. Hebrews 10:26-27 tell us that "if we deliberately keep on sinning after we have received the knowledge of the truth, no sacrifice for sins is left, but only a fearful expectation of judgment and of raging fire that will consume the enemies of God."

The longevity of God's Word as the compass to guide our worship is literally eternal: "Heaven and earth will pass away, but my words will never pass away" (Matthew 24:35). Romans 3:4 agrees: "Let God be true, and every human being a liar…" When it comes to the truth of God's Word versus the opinions of men—in every controversy of this type—man is a liar, and God's Word is true. The person who stubbornly goes on in the traditions of men while rejecting the Word of God automatically places himself under a closed heaven.

If you need to make a break with tradition, do as the Berean saints did. Acts 1:10-11 describes them: "As soon as it was night, the brothers sent Paul and Silas away to Berea. On arriving there, they went to the Jewish synagogue. Now the Berean Jews were of more noble character than those in Thessalonica, for they received the message with great eagerness and examined the Scriptures every day to see if what Paul said was true."

Search the Scriptures daily to be sure that the things you're learning in your church are truly from the Word of God. And stop being a man-pleaser—become a God pleaser instead. Be sure that you're following a good pastor who clearly teaches the Word of God rather than the traditions of men.

PART 2

[TEN STEPS TO FINANCIAL FREEDOM]

★ ★ ★ ★ ★

STEP #1—ACCESSING YOUR ABILITY TO GET WEALTH

I LIKE THE NIV VERSION OF DEUTERONOMY 8:18: "But remember the LORD your God, for it is he who gives you the ability to produce wealth, and so confirms his covenant, which he swore to your ancestors, as it is today." I like it because it says, "God has given us the ability to produce wealth."

When you look at the word "produce," what do you think of? I think of a production line or assembly line in a factory, where things are being manufactured. This automatically brings to mind a large number of people working on the line. This is where the first problem begins— many people want to live the lifestyle of the "rich and famous," but they do not want to *work* for wealth. God is not pleased with lazy people! The Word tells us that if a man does not work, he should not eat.

There are some people who will work, but they will not make any sacrifices to obtain wealth. Most people want to "get rich quick," but the Bible tells us that wealth comes slowly. The reason many people never become wealthy is because as soon as they begin to make more money, they change their lifestyle, and the new lifestyle consumes their increase.

Joyce Addis, whose testimony follows, is an example of Proverbs 3:9-10: "Honor the LORD with your wealth, with the firstfruits of all your crops; then your barns will be filled to overflowing, and your vats will brim over with new wine."

God has been so good to me and my family that I could never thank Him enough. God has blessed us beyond measure! With everything I say, I am bragging on God, not on anything that my husband and I have done.

My husband and I are both sixty years young, and we are still working. We have always worked hard, and God has honored our work ethic and blessed the work of our hands. People are always asking us when we plan to retire. Our answer is always the same: "We have no plans to retire." Where in God's Word does it tell us to retire when we reach a certain age, or obtain enough money?

We have been married twenty-six years, and both of us have been previously married. Between us, we have four children from our first marriages. The children are all grown and married, and we have seven grandchildren and two great-grandchildren. When we married, there were debts from our previous marriages which we wanted to get paid off.

My husband worked for his father in a plumbing business, and when his dad closed his business, he gave Tommy an old backhoe. Tommy used it to begin his first business— running sewer and water lines. If you know anything about construction, you know this is really hard work. He would work six, sometimes seven, days a week.

The tractor was old and always breaking down. There were many days he worked all day, something would break on the tractor, and he would work all night—or half of the night—so he would not miss any work the next day. When the weather was rainy and cold, there would be days he would come home from work, and the bottoms of his pant legs would be frozen stiff.

During this time, I worked for a truck line and would do all of my husband's paperwork at night and on the weekends. When we began to make money, we made plans to pay off our bills. Tommy desperately needed a newer tractor. We always lived on a budget. I never just went out and spent money, because I knew that, the next week, I would need that money for bills.

Every week, I had the money from my job, and Tommy gave me $300 for household bills and child support. Child support alone was $100 per week. Some weeks, if the weather was bad, Tommy might not make any money; but no matter how much or how little he made, he gave me the same amount each week. We never took any extra money out of Tommy's business—except at Christmas, and once a year for vacation.

As God began to prosper Tommy's business, he bought a newer backhoe. His business continued to increase, so he eventually bought two more backhoes and hired two people to run sewer and water lines for him. After a few years, he got to the point where he was able to buy new backhoes.

I had always gone to a Baptist church, but my husband was raised in a Pentecostal church. We began going to a Pentecostal church together. At that time, we began paying our tithes and offerings and have done so ever since. Let me say this: You can never expect God to bless you unless you give your tithes and offerings. Remember, nothing that we have belongs to us. Everything belongs to God, and we are only stewards of what God has entrusted to us.

When we married, Tommy was living in a house he had built with his first wife. A lot of my friends said, "You're not going to live in that house where his first wife lived, are you?" I laughed and told them that I would be sleeping with the man she slept with—so why did it matter where? There was a mortgage of $16,500 on the house, so we began to save money to pay it off. It wasn't too long until we were able to pay it in full. What a good feeling to have a home with no mortgage!

As Tommy's business grew, he needed a building, as we could not keep all of the equipment at our home. We bought an old rental house from his parents and gave the house to one of the men who worked for Tommy. He had the house moved to his property, where he repaired and lived in it. Tommy began to build a metal building on this lot. He paid a company to put the metal up, and he worked on the building on nights and weekends until it was finished. We were able to pay for this building as it was being built. We worked out of that building until January 2005.

A short time later, one of the builders we worked for had a small lot he wanted to sell. We bought the lot and constructed a building on it, which we leased. One day, a real estate agent came to our office and said he represented a major drug store chain. He proceeded to tell us that this chain was buying property, and they were going to blanket the Atlanta market with new stores. They'd bought a piece of property on a major roadway that joined our property, and they needed our property in order to be able to build on the lot they'd purchased. We decided to sell to them because they were offering us a really good price.

A couple weeks later, before any contracts were signed, the real estate agent came back and told us that the drug store chain had decided not to open any stores in Atlanta, and the deal was off. This was not a big problem for us, as we had tenants in the building. Then, about four to six weeks later, the same agent came back to our office and said the chain had now decided to build two stores in Atlanta...guess where one of them was going to be built? That's right—at the location that adjoined our property! So the deal was on again. This time, they gave us a contract, and we sold to them, making a good profit. Only God can do things like this for His children!

We were still living in the house Tommy owned when we married, but eventually, we wanted to move. Tommy had always wanted to live on a lake. One Saturday, a friend called and told him that some lots had been put up for sale on a lake in Fayetteville, Georgia. We went that day, looked at the lots, and ended up buying one the next week.

Everyone thought we'd lost our minds when we told them we purchased the lot and were going to build a new house. After we paid on the lot for a couple of years, Tommy began building our new home. He built a sixty-five-hundred-square-foot home. It was beautiful. We paid for it as we built it and ended up with a mortgage of only $111,000, which was not much at all.

In August of 1989, a gentleman Tommy knew called him and asked him to be a partner in a plumbing business he was getting ready to start. Tommy had been talking about going into the plumbing business for a while, so he agreed to partner with his friend. God blessed the business. It wasn't too long after it got up and running that we knew we would rather be on our own instead of having a partner.

We talked about approaching the partner about buying his share of the business, but we didn't know what to offer him— or if he would even want to sell. In just a short while, our partner came to Tommy and asked if we would buy his share of the business. Does God know how to take care of us or not? We told him we would buy him out, but first, we would get the accountant to evaluate the business and advise as to what his share was worth. However, he did not want to do that; he already knew what he wanted. The amount he asked for was a very small amount, and Tommy encouraged him to let us get an estimate from the accountant. Our partner would have no part of that. He simply wanted us to buy him out; so, within two weeks, we went to the closing and bought his share of the business.

After this, God opened a door for our business to begin working for a gentleman who owned a chain of extended-stay hotels. He was building these hotels all over the southeast. Tommy worked really hard, studied, and took tests to get his plumbing license in all of the states where this company was building. We worked for them several years, and God really did bless our business during this time. The owner would give us raises without us even asking. We worked for this company until the owner sold the business. God gave Tommy favor with this gentleman, and they still keep in touch with each other today.

It was during this time that we decided to pay off our mortgage. We began sending extra money each month when we made our monthly payments and, seven years after we moved into our new home, we had paid it off.

We had a beautiful home and yard, but we were in a small subdivision and decided we wanted to move to a place with a little acreage where we wouldn't be so close to other people. One day, as Tommy was going to work, he passed some property with a newly-erected "For Sale" sign. He called the number and, the next day, we met the owner and walked over the 17.5-acre property. The owner was not asking much, considering it was in Fayette County. We told him we would buy the property, and he asked when we could close on it. We told him we would close the following week, and believe it or not, he ended up lowering the price. After we closed on the property, we had two ponds put on the land that was going to be our new home site.

We began construction on our new home and worked for a few months before the Lord moved on Tommy's heart to build a new church. Work on our new home stopped as Tommy worked on the church for the next year. While he did this, he did not charge the church anything for his time or labor.

Once the church was complete, he went back to building our new home. After about a year, he almost had it ready, but we had a small problem: the house we were living in had been on the market for about eighteen months, and it had not sold. During this time, we had actually gotten one contract on the house, but it seemed as though the prospective buyer could not be satisfied. She compiled a list about two pages long of things she wanted changed. I knew she would be one of those people who would be hard to satisfy, so I asked the Lord to change her mind about buying the house if there were going to be problems.

The very next week, the real estate agent called and said the potential buyer wanted out of the contract. She told me that, legally, we could keep the $10,000 she had put down as earnest money. I told the agent that not only would I be happy to release her from the contract, but I would also give the earnest money back! So there we sat, with no buyer for our home, and the new house about to be ready in four to six weeks. But you know what? God is never late! It wasn't long before He sent an engaged couple to look at our home. They ended up signing a contract to purchase it.

The following Monday evening, the doorbell rang, and there stood the couple who was purchasing our home. They said they were not trying to do anything unethical, but just wanted to talk to us about the house. They had prayed all weekend about this purchase, and the Lord had told them to buy our home and to pay us the asking price. The only thing they asked us to do was have the carpet professionally cleaned when we moved out. Not only did we do that, but we also had the trim on the outside of the house painted. When we moved, I had the house and all the windows cleaned for them. We've formed a friendship with this beautiful couple, and they have been a blessing to both us and our church.

So God sent us the right people at the right time to buy our house! We were able to move into our new home without the worry of having a vacant house sitting waiting to be sold. Why do we worry and fret about things? God is in control of everything and will always work things out for us if we will simply let Him.

Our new home, which is approximately 15,000 square feet, sits on the 17.5 acres we purchased. It sits a good distance off the street, and it is a beauty! We had it professionally decorated and the grounds professionally landscaped. God has been so good to us!

I have often wondered why God chose to bless us the way He has. I do not know the answer to that question, but I do know that we are grateful for His blessings. My husband and I have always been—and still are—hard workers. We have always paid our tithes and offerings and tried to help people in any way we can. Also, we understand that nothing we have belongs to us. It all belongs to God. He has allowed us to be stewards over everything we have, and we try to please Him with our stewardship.

JESUS AND THE WEALTH OF THE WICKED

Every material possession God ever gave His children came from the wicked. Even the Promised Land that He gave Abraham was the bona fide possession of someone else. When Sarah died, Abraham buried her on the land God had given him. However, he had to pay cash for the burial site. While there is no question God had given him the land, Abraham had not yet taken possession of it.

God also took the wealth of the wicked Egyptians and gave it to His children when He brought them out of captivity. This same thing happened time after time throughout the Old Testament. You don't have to go far in studying the Bible before you realize that God continually strips the wicked of their wealth and gives it to His children:

Proverbs 13:22: "A good person leaves an inheritance for their children's children, but a sinner's wealth is stored up for the righteous."

Proverbs 28:8: "Whoever increases wealth by taking interest or profit from the poor amasses it for another, who will be kind to the poor."

Ecclesiastes 2:26: "To the person who pleases him, God gives wisdom, knowledge and happiness, but to the sinner he gives the task of gathering and storing up wealth to hand it over to the one who pleases God. This too is meaningless, a chasing after the wind."

Job 27:13, 16-17: "Here is the fate God allots to the wicked, the heritage a ruthless man receives from the Almighty...Though he heaps up silver like dust and clothes like piles of clay, what he lays up the righteous will wear, and the innocent will divide his silver."

These Scriptures are crystal clear. They declare God's intention to give the wealth of the sinner to His righteous children. While everyone agrees that the Old Testament teaches this truth, is it still true for us today?

IT'S FOR TODAY

Jesus does speak of transferring wealth from the wicked to the just. One of the strongest instances is found in Mark 4:25: "Whoever has will be given more; whoever does not have, even what they have will be taken from them."

In this verse, Jesus is speaking of two groups: those who have and those who have not. To understand what the "haves" have and the "have-nots" don't have, you must strictly adhere to the biblical context of this verse. Upon close examination, you will find that, in the preceding verses, the subject never changes. Be careful, though, for Mark sometimes states the subject, and other times he implies it. However, it does not change. The subject remains "understanding."

The most effective way to show you what our Lord is actually saying in verse 25 is to paraphrase the preceding verses of Mark 4:23-25: "'If any man has ears to understand, let him understand...Be careful what you understand, for with the same measure of understanding you do your giving, God will measure your return back to you. The more understanding you have, the greater your return will be, for he who has understanding will receive, and he who doesn't have understanding, even the wealth he has will be taken from him."

When these verses are written out in this way, it's easy to see that the Lord is speaking of taking possessions from one group and giving them to the other. In Mark 4:10-12, He identifies one group as having understanding and the other as not having it: "When he was alone, the Twelve and the others around him asked him about the parables. He told them, 'The secret of the kingdom of God has been given to you. But to those on the outside everything is said in parables so that, "they may be ever seeing but never perceiving, and ever hearing but never understanding; otherwise they might turn and be forgiven!"'"

The Lord makes it clear who understands and who doesn't. When He is alone with the disciples, they ask about the meaning of the parable of the sower. He tells them they (the children of God) can know (understand) the mysteries of the Kingdom of God, but outsiders (the children of darkness) can't know (understand) them. Verse 12 puts it plainly—Jesus simply says He will give the possessions of those who don't understand the Kingdom of God (the wicked) to those who do understand it (those who are righteous in His sight).

In Mark 4:24, Jesus is actually paraphrasing the second part of Proverbs 13:22: "A sinner's wealth is stored up for the righteous." The words of this verse become so clear when we understand Mark 4:23-25 in its Scriptural context! Jesus is simply telling us where God is temporarily storing the abundance He wants to give us. At the moment, it is in the hands of the wicked. They have it stacked up and rusting, awaiting the end of time, when God will redistribute it to His children. God plans to give us the wealth that the wicked now possess.

TWO OTHER PLACES

Jesus plainly states in two other places that God will give the wealth of the wicked to the just. One instance is in the sixth chapter of Matthew, where He tells us of the benefits of seeking His Kingdom first. Upon close examination of the context of this verse, you will find that Jesus promises to add the very same things the Gentiles (sinners) are seeking to stack up to those who seek first the Kingdom of God and His righteousness.

Jesus is saying to us, "Seek first the kingdom of God and His righteousness, and all the things the sinners are stacking up, God will subtract from them and add to you." Jesus also declares that God will give the wealth of the wicked to the just through the Parable of the Talents in Matthew 25:26-28.

If you remember, the master in this parable gives five talents to one servant, two talents to another, and one to the last. Two of these servants are faithful to obey the master and increase their talents. However, the third servant hides his talents in the ground. When the master comes to reckon with this disobedient servant, the master says, "Thou wicked and slothful servant...Take therefore the talent from him, and give it unto him which hath ten talents" (verse 26, 28, KJV).

Thank God that the mega-wealth the wicked now possess is once again ready to change hands. No longer will it stagnate in their treasure houses. It is even now ready for redistribution among the informed children of God.

WEALTH NEVER LIES IN THE STREETS

These words from the lips of our Lord bring much credibility to the message of manifesting superabundance, for everyone knows that wealth never lies in the streets. It's always in someone's possession. God will simply take it from the wicked as He has done in times past, and give it to His children. Remember, if He has done it before, you can depend upon Him doing it again: according to Hebrews 13:8, "Jesus Christ is the same yesterday and today and forever." There is more wealth in the world today than ever before. It's out there right now, waiting for that special end-time group of Christians who will understand enough about biblical economics to acquire and use it.

A PROCESS, NOT AN EVENT

Looking back to Mark 24, notice how smoothly our Lord changes the subject from transferring the wealth from the wicked to the just to the timing involved in manifesting the wealth transfer: Jesus tells us that abundance by biblical principles comes in the same way the farmer's harvest does.

We all know that bringing a seed to harvest is not an instantaneous event. It's a time-consuming process. God's abundant supply comes from a lifestyle of sowing that steadily progresses from stage to stage. Each time of sowing brings more abundance, until the final phase, which is exceedingly abundant—above all you can ask or think (Ephesians 3:20).

★ ★ ★ ★ ★

STEP #2—ACCEPTING YOUR RESPONSIBILITY OF TITHING

TWO SEPARATE FAMILIES IN A CHURCH BEGIN TO TITHE

SOMETIMES, ONE FAMILY EXPERIENCES AN INCREASE IN their income, while another family sees no change. After a while, the family who has seen no results begins to complain and question the Word of God. They begin to accuse God of not prospering them as He is prospering other tithers. The truth is that there is nothing wrong with God. He is not a respecter of persons (Acts 10:34). His heart's desire is to prosper both families as much as they will allow.

You will find, upon closer observation of such families, that one family prospers because it has a solid understanding of God's Word and what He expects from them. The solution for the other family is simple: its members have to get into God's Word. They have to increase their understanding of His qualifications for receiving through the open heaven their tithe had created (Malachi 3:10). Most people don't fully understand, but at least twenty-five things—the things we've just explored in the first portion of this book—can immediately block the flow from heaven to a tither. It is imperative that you remember the words of our Lord. If you wish to increase your receiving, you must increase your understanding.

Remember: If any man has ears to understand, let him understand. Jesus said it again and again to those He spoke to during His time on earth. Be careful what you understand, because God will give more to those who properly understand (Mark 4:23-24, paraphrased).

Often, people have been taught not to expect anything back when they give to God; but if a farmer plants corn, he has the right to expect a harvest of corn. Likewise, you can expect a harvest when you give to God.

FARMER JOHN

Suppose I decided to move to a farm and make my living there for ten years. On this farm would be everything a farmer needs: tools, seed, fertilizer, books about farming, and information on the time and location of weekly classes on proper farming.

If I were to pay close attention to the lectures and totally believe what the textbook on farming said, I might have a harvest in the first year. Yet, if I did, it would no doubt be a limited one. If I were to continue to study and attend the lectures, faithfully applying every new thing I understood about farming, surely my harvest would increase each year.

Why would this increase occur? It wouldn't be because attending lectures on farming makes me lucky. No—it would be because the more I study farming, the more my understanding of what to do increases. The more I understand and follow good advice, the more harvest the good ground of that farm will yield to me. This same principle applies to your giving to God. With each bit of Scriptural understanding you gain, you will automatically increase your ability to receive.

I imagine you're familiar with a disease that afflicts some people called cirrhosis of the liver. It occurs when one's liver has been damaged by any number of causes. The liver hardens because of the excessive formation of connective tissue followed by contractions. However, have you ever heard of the disease called "Cirrhosis of the Giver?" It has hit the population particularly harshly since the beginning of the twentieth century. It is an acute condition which renders the patient's hand immobile when it attempts to move from the billfold to the offering plate. The only remedy is to remove the afflicted from the house of God, since it has been clinically observed that this condition disappears in alternate environments such as golf courses, nightclubs, or restaurants.

The first recorded case actually occurred about 34 AD. It proved terminal in a couple named Ananias and Sapphira, whom we studied at the beginning of this book. Their story is a direct contrast to another story about a man who died and went to heaven. There, he made this comment concerning his use of money on earth: "What I spent, I lost. What I saved, I left. And what I gave, I have."

We do not lose what we give. We send it on before us, that we may have treasure in heaven. Jesus made this clear in Matthew 6:19-21: "Do not store up for yourselves treasures on earth, where moth and rust destroy, and where thieves break in and steal. But store up for yourselves treasures in heaven, where moth and rust do not destroy, and where thieves do not break in and steal. For where your treasure is, there your heart will be also."

Unless it's for our own pleasure, humans have traditionally resisted surrendering their hard-earned money. Consider Matthew 22:15-21:

> Then the Pharisees went out and laid plans to trap him in his words. They sent their disciples to him along with the Herodians. "Teacher," they said, "we know that you are a man of integrity and that you teach the way of God in accordance with the truth. You aren't swayed by others, because you pay no attention to who they are. Tell us then, what is your opinion? Is it right to pay the imperial tax to Caesar or not?"

But Jesus, knowing their evil intent, said, "You hypocrites, why are you trying to trap me? Show me the coin used for paying the tax." They brought him a denarius, and he asked them, "Whose image is this? And whose inscription?"

"Caesar's," they replied.

Then he said to them, "So give back to Caesar what is Caesar's, and to God what is God's."

We in the 21st century aren't much different. We don't like to pay taxes, but we like driving on good roads and highways. We don't like to pay taxes, but we like for our children to be in good schools. We don't like to pay taxes, but we like to draw a check at retirement—even if it is not enough.

Before the Roman government oppressed them, the ancient Israelites resisted giving their money even to their spiritual authority. Consider Malachi 3:8-12:

"Will a mere mortal rob God? Yet you rob me.

"But you ask, 'How are we robbing you?'

"In tithes and offerings. You are under a curse—your whole nation—because you are robbing me. Bring the whole tithe into the storehouse, that there may be food in my house. Test me in this," says the Lord Almighty, "and see if I will not throw open the floodgates of heaven and pour out so much blessing that there will not be room enough to store it. I will prevent pests from devouring your crops, and the vines in your fields will not drop their fruit before it is ripe," says the Lord Almighty. "Then all the nations will call you blessed, for yours will be a delightful land," says the Lord Almighty.

Once again, we aren't much different. We don't like to give, but we like being recipients of God's promises. We don't like to give, but we want God's healing. We don't like to give, but we want God's abundant blessing. We don't like to give, but we want all of our needs to be met.

Perhaps we would have the desires of our hearts if we took to heart Luke 6:37-38: "Do not judge, and you will not be judged. Do not condemn, and you will not be condemned. Forgive, and you will be forgiven. Give, and it will be given to you. A good measure, pressed down, shaken together and running over, will be poured into your lap. For with the measure you use, it will be measured to you."

STEP #3—ALLOWING THE GREAT PHYSICIAN TO DO PLASTIC SURGERY

YOU'VE CHARGED IT UP—NOW, IT'S PAY-DOWN TIME. You may feel like you're in over your head and there is no way to reverse the damage you've done to your finances through credit card debt. But with wisdom and God's help, there is something you can do. Here is the personal testimony of our associate pastor, Angela Batemon:

> In November of 1999, I attended a debt-free class at Living Faith Tabernacle. Through that class, I was delivered from the thought that constantly plagued me: *You will always be in financial bondage.* The teachers, Tommy and Joyce Addis, taught about budgets, and other attendees testified of how they were working on becoming debt-free. I was never taught that you could be debt-free; I was never taught about paying off bills, cars, and houses. After I heard that God's will was for us to be lenders and not borrowers, I left the class

motivated to become debt-free. I shared the vision with my husband, and we immediately began to put the class's principles into action. We started with Habakkuk 2:2 (KJV): "And the Lord answered me and said, Write the vision, and make it plain upon tables, that he may run that readeth it." My husband and I sat down and wrote down all of our creditors (to our surprise, we had 21 of them!) and what we owed (also to our surprise, we were paying thousands of dollars in interest each month!). We destroyed every credit card except for one, which we keep for emergency purposes only. Then, we put what we learned—the Dump Theory—into action. Over a three-year period, we paid off all of our creditors with the exception of our mortgage company. Because we practiced what we learned, our credit scores have soared.

Today, we can proudly say that God has made us the lender. Through the teachings we received, we were able to take the money we were giving to our creditors and use it to buy stock in some of the same companies we were once slaves to. We are also able to freely give to the work of the Lord. We have been blessed beyond measure in our finances. Thank God for Living Faith Tabernacle, Pastor Chris Bowen, and Tommy and Joyce Addis. They share their wisdom so freely with so many.

If you're up to your eyeballs in credit card and other debt—paying the minimums and little else—it's time to get serious. The best way to get rid of debt, experts agree, is to attack the balance with the highest annual percentage rate first. When that is paid off, move on to the debt with the next-highest interest rate.

It is imperative, though, that you always attack that highest-interest debt first. On that debt, you want to "double, triple, quadruple minimum payments," says Howard S. Dvorkin, president and founder of Consolidated Credit Counseling Services in Fort Lauderdale, Florida. "When you're done with that one, move on to the next one. The amount you owe doesn't really matter when you're paying an enormous amount of interest. Try to pay the highest interest rate ones first. Muster all the funds available and get the debt out of your life."

However, there is an alternative plan which allows you to pay the smallest debt FIRST. This allows you to minimize overall the number of companies you owe. Wouldn't it make you feel better to knock off some low-balance bills first and eliminate a bill or two from that thick monthly pile? You may use this plan if you feel that it will give you the boost you need to stick with a paydown plan.

"It makes better financial sense to pay down the highest interest rate first. But people get discouraged. So they knock down lower balances first," says Steve Rhode, co-founder of the nonprofit financial services organization Myvesta. "It's a lot more gratifying for some people to pay off the smaller balances within a couple months. They feel like they're making more progress." However, once those smaller balances are gone, go back to Plan A: take the money set aside to pay those bills and apply it to the balance with the highest interest rate. Gather all the funds available, and get the debt out of your life once and for all. Once you've tasted life without credit card debt, I assure you that you'll never want to go back. According to Proverbs 22:7, "The rich rule over the poor, and the borrower is servant to the lender." We should owe no man.

Two things determine how our money is spent: our priorities and our self-control. One of the main elements to your "plastic surgery success" is that you stick to your plan! The key to an effective paydown plan is not giving up. Don't let up on the monthly payments as your minimums inch down and as bills get paid off. Aren't you ready for your financial freedom? You can never have it until you go through surgery—PLASTIC SURGERY!

The statistics are depressing:
- Consumer debt in the United States has topped $2 trillion.
- There are over 600 million credit cards in the United States today.
- For every dollar earned, the average American family spends $1.22.

- There are 5 billion offers for credit cards mailed out each year.
- College students now leave school with an average of three credit cards.

Take a look at three Scriptures that are the foundation to the principle of going through this type of surgery. Taken together, they are a compelling argument for the eternal importance of debt management and good stewardship: Ephesians 2:10 says, "For we are God's handiwork, created in Christ Jesus to do good works, which God prepared in advance for us to do." We are each sent here to accomplish specific good works. I can't accomplish yours, and you can't accomplish mine. In Revelation 22:12, Jesus says, "Look, I am coming soon! My reward is with me, and I will give to each person according to what they have done." There will come a day when we will stand before the Lord and answer for accomplishing or not accomplishing those good works, and we will be rewarded accordingly. Lastly, 1 Corinthians 3:12-15 states, "If anyone builds on this foundation using gold, silver, costly stones, wood, hay or straw, their work will be shown for what it is, because the Day will bring it to light. It will be revealed with fire, and the fire will test the quality of each person's work. If what has been built survives, the builder will receive a reward. If it is burned up, the builder will suffer loss but yet will be saved—even though only as one escaping through the flames."

Let me be very clear: I'm not talking about salvation. That is received through the blood of Christ alone. I am talking about the eternal rewards we will or won't receive based on what we've accomplished on earth. Far too many are unable to accomplish what the Lord sent them here to do because they are enslaved by debt. The result is that they will have stored little or no eternal rewards on the other side. Debt will have robbed them not only in this world, but also in the one to come.

Basically, there are two types of debt: long-term debt and short-term (also known as consumer) debt. Long-term debt is usually associated with an asset that has significant value. The classic example is a home mortgage: you borrow money to purchase a house and have debt, but you also have something of value. In the worst-case scenario, you can sell the house, pay off the mortgage, and no longer have that debt. People don't usually get into financial trouble over their long-term debts. On the other hand, short-term debt is usually associated with something quickly consumed—meals, vacations, clothes, entertainment, and a variety of other niceties that are soon forgotten, while the associated debt seems to linger forever. This type of debt primarily consists of credit card debt, but it could also include any loan that has no valuable asset associated with it, such as a consolidation loan, a home equity loan, or a credit union loan. Poorly stewarded short-term debt has the ability to make us less able to be used by God.

The following symptoms indicate that your short-term debt is out of control:

- You never have enough money to get to the end of the month.
- You have nothing saved for emergencies.
- You charge items to delay having to pay for them.
- You continually "roll" your debt from one credit card to another.
- You consolidate loans to pay off credit card debt.
- Your combined debts consume more than 35 percent of your gross income.
- Your car note is greater than 15 percent of your take-home pay.
- You have been late on any payment in the last six months.
- You don't really how much you owe.

If you find yourself in this situation, take these steps immediately:

- Confess your mess: Repent and ask the Lord for forgiveness for your poor stewardship. Then, commit your finances to Him and His ways.
- Have plastic surgery: Cut up your credit cards immediately. Cancel all of your accounts.
- Develop a written plan to get totally out of debt. Write your list down, and post it where everyone in the family will see it.

Create a graph of your debts and post it where you will be able to see them decrease each month.

- Start by paying off your highest interest rate credit card first, while continuing to make the minimum payments on your other debts. Once one card is paid off, double the payments on the next card. Continue this until all of your cards are paid off.
- Pay cash. Studies show that, if you pay cash for your purchases, you will actually spend 30-40 percent less each month. Imagine how quickly you could pay off your debts with this 30-40 percent raise.
- Wait twenty-four hours before making most purchases. 80 percent of all purchases are made on impulse. Good things come to those who wait.
- Seek wise financial counsel from someone who has nothing to gain from you.
- Learn to hate consumer debt as if it were Satan himself. In many cases, debt is the enemy's primary weapon for rendering us useless to the Kingdom of God.

When people seriously commit to stewardship, they can expect slow starts and supernatural suddenlies:

- They consistently do the right thing, regardless of the short-term cost.
- Their stewardship is tested both in the natural and the supernatural realms.
- As they stay the course, as well as follow God's instructions on giving, the windows of heaven open up on them and supernatural suddenlies are poured out: They receive new jobs and raises, debts are forgiven, and money comes from unexpected sources.

Today is the day to commit to taking back dominion over your finances. As you succeed, God will reveal to you benefits that are out of this world!

* ★ ★ ★ ★ ★ *

STEP #4—ACQUIRING A TASTE FOR GOOD STEWARDSHIP

STEWARDSHIP IS NOT ABOUT GIVING OR EVEN about giving more. It's about arranging our finances in such a way that they reflect the fact that everything belongs to God, everything comes from God, and everything is disbursed by God.

This is true based on Proverbs 22:2-3: "Rich and poor have this in common: The LORD is the Maker of them all. The prudent see danger and take refuge, but the simple keep going and pay the penalty."

There are five things you do with your money that can lead to bad stewardship:

- Spend it.
- Repay debt.
- Pay taxes.
- Save it.
- Give it.

If you have an "ownership" mentality toward your finances, you will base your priorities accordingly: "I'm the king of my life, and I'm king of my financial world. Therefore, I will:

- Spend my money the way I want to spend it.
- Pay my bills so I won't go to jail.
- Pay as few taxes as I can without going to jail.
- Save some—if I'm smart.
- Give some if there is a real tear-jerking cause, and if I have a lot of money so that I can spare a few dollars."

When prioritizing in this way, you are giving God the LEFT-OVERS! God gets what is leftover after you meet your own agenda. However, when you act as steward rather than owner, you never give God leftovers.

THE UNJUST STEWARD

As Christ relates to us the parable of the unjust steward in Luke 16, we must not forget what had come before. In chapter 15, Jesus rebuked the Pharisees for their lack of love for the lost. Using three parables, He illustrated the love of God for sinners and spoke of joy in heaven when even one sinner repents.

The Pharisees had been given stewardship—they had been entrusted with the Word of God, the Old Testament Scriptures and the Gospel. Their Master, God, had put them in charge of teaching, shepherding, and comforting His sheep with His Word. Instead, they took care of themselves. They partook of the fruit of labors they did not perform and pretended to be lovers of God and His law. They neglected and, in fact, despised God's lost sheep.

As we study the parable of the unjust steward, remember that the Pharisees were still very likely within earshot, even though Jesus was primarily talking to His disciples. According to this parable, they were (and we are) called to practice good stewardship. As you will see, this stewardship encompasses all that we are, have, and do.

> Now He was also saying to the disciples, "There was a rich man who had a manager, and this manager was reported to him as squandering his possessions. And he called him and said to him, 'What is this I hear about you? Give an

accounting of your management, for you can no longer be manager.' The manager said to himself, 'What shall I do, since my master is taking the management away from me? I am not strong enough to dig; I am ashamed to beg. I know what I shall do, so that when I am removed from the management people will welcome me into their homes.' (Luke 16:1-4, NASB)

The Strong's Greek dictionary defines the word "steward" as follows: "To manage; the manager of a household, or a treasurer." Webster says of the same, "A steward is a person who manages another's property, finances, or other affairs. A person in charge of the household affairs of a large estate, club, hotel or resort."

A steward, then, is a person trusted by another—his master or employer—to manage treasure, business, or livelihood. On the human and material side of things, an unjust steward could bring his master to poverty or bankruptcy. Surely, we can see the seriousness of the situation described in the parable.

This man was trusted implicitly with the master's money. Instead of being frugal and wise on his master's behalf, he squandered the master's resources. The word "squander" conveys the idea of scattering, as in sowing seed to the four winds. In other words, this man wasted, spent, gave away, or did not collect his masters money as he'd been hired to do. He was at least a poor manager, and likely an out-and-out thief.

We are not surprised to hear that he is fired. His days of living "high on the hog" at the expense of his master are over. What will he do for a living? How will he survive? He is, in his own estimation, too weak to dig and would be ashamed to beg. What can he do? Well, he decides to make his master's debtors beholden to him so that, when he finds himself in need, he will have someone who owes him a favor:

And he summoned each one of his master's debtors, and he began saying to the first, 'How much do you owe my master?' And he said, 'A hundred measures of oil.' And he said to him, 'Take your bill, and sit down quickly and write fifty.' Then he said to another, 'And how much do you owe?' And he said, 'A hundred measures of wheat.' He said to him, 'Take your bill, and write eighty.'

Can you believe it? This man has no conscience! He cost his master dearly while he worked for him, and he continues to rob him after he's fired! He has no right to discount these people's debts! He has no right to mess with what is owed to another! This man is an unjust steward—a thief! But he's not a *dumb* thief. On the contrary, he is quite clever—something which the master notices right away in verse 8:

> And his master praised the unrighteous steward because he had acted shrewdly; (He praised him for his ingenuity, cleverness, and prudence in concocting a way to get food and shelter after he has lost his job. He was not praising him for his dishonesty; he fired him for that.)

From this point on, Jesus begins to apply the parable to all who hear—specifically the disciples. They were (and we are) to look at this creative unbeliever and learn something. But what? It has to do with stewardship: with using our time, talents, and money in a way that pleases our Master, God. The parable has to do with honesty, faithfulness, prudence, and shrewdness in living the Christian life. Why? The end of verse 8 tells us: "For the sons of this age (non-Christians) are more shrewd in relation to their own kind than the sons of light (Christians)."

Jesus points out something that hasn't changed to this day: unbelievers all too often exhibit more forethought, wisdom, prudence, shrewdness, dedication, and determination in the way they pursue their various interests than Christians do.

For instance, the football fan will often forsake his family and friends to watch or attend a game. Meanwhile, the Christian may only attend the scheduled worship services of the church if there is nothing better to do. The football fan is often seen sitting in the rain to watch a game, while the slightest hint of inclement weather may very well keep the Christian home from church.

The serious, unbelieving fishermen will spend thousands of dollars on first-class equipment so he can enjoy his sport. He devotes time and energy to learning the lakes, the water temperature, and the behavior of the fish so he can be a successful fisherman. The Christian, on the other hand, may devote little or no money to his spiritual pursuits. Neither does he train himself with Bible study or corporate worship and fellowship with other believers. There are various tools he could purchase that would help him understand the Scriptures more clearly, but he has better places to put his money and better ways to use his time.

The unbeliever is often shrewd and thoughtful when investing his money, while it is not uncommon for the Christian to be careless and haphazard in the use of the money God gives him. The unbeliever will often work hard for a promotion so he can better care for his family or give more to his particular political party or favorite charity, while the Christian too often performs his duties on the job in a disinterested, mediocre fashion and then complains about being passed over at promotion time. The unbeliever will diligently recruit people to his cause, political persuasion, club, or organization. On the other hand, some Christians don't even seem to care if anyone goes to heaven but them. These comparisons could go on and on.

Look around you, ladies and gentlemen. What you see is the world charging ahead with determination and careful calculation. Though they are really headed nowhere, you see them using every means and resource at their disposal to get there. They will stop at nothing to reach their goals and fulfill their dreams. Yes, they are motivated by the lust of their eyes and the pride of life...but look at them go. Surely, those who are called to and want to live for the glory of God should be at least as determined and diligent as they are!

As believers in Jesus and worshipers of the one true God, we need to be shrewd, prudent, wise, and dedicated to working out our Christianity in the most God-honoring and profitable way possible.

For we have been entrusted with both physical and spiritual steward-ship. The Scriptures speak of both.

1 Corinthians 4:1-2 (NASB) says, "Let a man regard us in this manner, as servants of Christ and stewards of the mysteries of God. In this case, moreover, it is required of stewards that one be found trustworthy." This text has to do with ministers, but all Christians are stewards of the truth they've had revealed to them.

And don't forget our responsibility to steward the gifts given to us—we see this in 1 Peter 4:7-10 (NASB): "The end of all things is near; therefore, be of sound judgment and sober spirit for the pur-pose of prayer. Above all, keep fervent in your love for one another, because love covers a multitude of sins. Be hospitable to one another without complaint. As each one has received a special gift, employ it in serving one another as good stewards of the manifold grace of God."

May it never be said of us what was said of the people of Israel in Jeremiah 4:22 (NASB): "For My people are foolish, they know Me not; they are stupid children, and they have no understanding. They are shrewd to do evil, but to do good they do not know."

As stewards of the manifold grace of God, let us be as clever in the pursuit of righteousness, holiness, growth in grace and knowl-edge, and general spiritual health as the unbeliever is in the pursuit of evil. Let us make good use of the time, talents, energy, and graces given to us by God. Let us make much use of the means of grace at our disposal. I speak of private Bible reading and prayer. I speak of corporate worship, Bible study, prayer, and fellowship. These are the disciplines that will help us become better stewards of the manifold grace of God entrusted to each believer.

We are also to be good stewards of the physical things God trusts us with, according to Proverbs 27:23-27.

> Know well the condition of your flocks, and pay atten-tion to your herds; for riches are not forever, nor does a crown endure to all generations. When the grass disappears, the new growth is seen, and the herbs of the mountains are

gathered in, the lambs will be for your clothing, and the goats will bring the price of a field, and there will be goats' milk enough for your food, for the food of your household, and sustenance for your maidens.

If you do not take care of your job—be it shepherding or rocket science—you will not have it for long. Therefore, there will not be enough food for your household. The Christian who works at his job with the awareness that it was given to him by God to care for and manage well will be the best employee or employer around, for by this job, he glorifies God, and by this job, God provides his material needs.

Remember, as an employee, you have been entrusted with your master's (employer's/company's) treasure, money, or income. You can either help or harm the man/business. His goods are not yours to do with as you please. His time is not yours to do with as you please. You and I are stewards only, whether of the things of God or of the things that belong to our earthly masters. We must be good stewards on both counts.

No matter what human we work for or how hard a character he might be, we must perform our duties for the Lord. Colossians 3:22-24 (NASB) directs us in this way: "Slaves, (employees) in all things obey those who are your masters on earth, not with external service, as those who merely please men, but with sincerity of heart, fearing the Lord. Whatever you do, do your work heartily, as for the Lord rather than for men; knowing that from the Lord you will receive the reward of the inheritance. It is the Lord Christ whom you serve."

When a person serves Christ by being a good and faithful steward of his job, he will be blessed with enough for himself and for others as well. Ephesians 4:28 (NASB) encourages, "He who steals must steal no longer; but rather he must labor, performing with his own hands what is good, so that he will have something to share with one who has need."

If you have been an unjust steward, it is time for reform. If you have been accustomed to stealing from the company you work for, it is time to stop. Stop stealing your employer's goods and the time you are paid for. Begin now to labor hard for the glory of God, your own needs, the needs of others, and the good of your employer. Be a good and faithful steward.

CAN MONEY BE YOUR FRIEND?

One of the most difficult statements Christ ever made was in Luke 16:9 (NASB): "And I say to you, make friends for yourselves by means of the wealth of unrighteousness, so that when it fails, they will receive you into the eternal dwellings."

What does this mean? If you press the details of the verse too hard, you will come up with something Christ never intended to teach—something like, "Make friends by giving them money so that, when you die, those who have gone before you will welcome you into heaven." Some respected commentators actually believe that is what Christ said and meant. I don't think so.

What one needs to do is hold the parable at arm's-length to view the whole thing at once. As I did this, I was inclined to agree with J. C. Ryle, who said, "The expression (the words of verse nine) appears to me to be general and indefinite, and to be borrowed from the conduct of the unjust steward, in order to make the lesson more pointed. The meaning seems to me to be no more than this. 'Use your money with an eye to the future, as the steward did his. Spend your money in such a way that your expenditure shall be a friend to you, and not a witness against you in another world.' This is the meaning of Christ's statement."

We are to use our money so that it does us good and so it is not a witness against us. We do this by using our money for the glory of God. We do that by using it according to the instructions given to us in the Bible. Here are a few examples.

In answer to a question about paying taxes to the government, Jesus says to his disciples, "'Show me the coin used for the poll-tax.' And they brought Him a denarius. And He said to them, 'Whose likeness and inscription is this?' They said to Him, 'Caesar's.' Then He said to them, 'Then render to Caesar the things that are Caesar's; and to God the things that are God's'" (Matthew 22:19-21, NASB).

Paul says, "For rulers are not a cause of fear for good behavior, but for evil. Do you want to have no fear of authority? Do what is good and you will have praise from the same; for it is a minister of God to you for good. But if you do what is evil, be afraid; for it does not bear the sword for nothing; for it is a minister of God, an avenger who brings wrath on the one who practices evil. Therefore it is necessary to be in subjection, not only because of wrath, but also for conscience' sake. For because of this you also pay taxes, for rulers are servants of God, devoting themselves to this very thing. Render to all what is due them: tax to whom tax is due; custom to whom custom; fear to whom fear; honor to whom honor" (Romans 13:3-7, NASB).

Good stewardship involves the cheerful support of our government. It also involves financially supporting the church, or giving to God. Giving to the church or to the Lord's work is not an option. However, the amount one gives to God is determined by the individual.

Hear the Word of the Lord in 2 Corinthians 9:6-11 (NASB): "Now this I say, he who sows sparingly will also reap sparingly; and he who sows bountifully will also reap bountifully. Each one must do (give) just as he has purposed in his heart; not grudgingly or under compulsion; for God loves a cheerful giver. . . Now He who supplies seed to the sower and bread for food will supply and multiply your seed for sowing and increase the harvest of your righteousness; you will be enriched in everything for all liberality, which through us is producing thanksgiving to God."

Those who have a heart for giving to the Lord and His work often say things like 1 Chronicles 29:14-17:

> But who am I, and what is my people, that we should be able to offer so willingly after this sort? For all things come of thee, and of thine own have we given thee.

For we are strangers before thee, and sojourners, as were all our fathers: our days on the earth are as a shadow, and there is none abiding.

O Lord our God, all this store that we have prepared to build thee an house for thine holy name cometh of thine hand, and is all thine own.

I know also, my God, that thou triest the heart, and hast pleasure in uprightness. As for me, in the uprightness of mine heart I have willingly offered all these things: and now have I seen with joy thy people, which are present here, to offer willingly unto thee. (KJV)

I once owed a man $2,000 and wondered how I would pay him back. It wasn't long before I received a gift from the same man for more than what I owed him. I paid him back with his own money! When we give to the Lord, we are simply returning what He gave us in the first place. We are merely overseers of what has always belonged to the Lord. How generous we ought to be when giving back to Him!

As stewards of the money God gives us, we are also to support the poor. Proverbs 19:17 (NASB) says, "One who is gracious to a poor man lends to the LORD, and He will repay him for his good deed." And Proverbs 28:27 (NASB) says, "He who gives to the poor will never want, but he who shuts his eyes will have many curses."

Deuteronomy 15:7-8 (NASB) also makes this clear: "If there is a poor man with you, one of your brothers, in any of your towns in your land which the LORD your God is giving you, you shall not harden your heart, nor close your hand from your poor brother; but you shall freely open your hand to him, and shall generously lend him sufficient for his need in whatever he lacks."

The New Testament makes no exception. We find the same instruction in 1 Timothy 6:17-19 (NASB):

Instruct those who are rich in this present world not to be conceited or to fix their hope on the uncertainty of riches, but on God, who richly supplies us with all things to enjoy. Instruct them to do good, to be rich in good works, to be generous and ready to share, storing up for themselves the treasure of a good foundation for the future, so that they may take hold of that which is life indeed.

Verse 19—"storing up for themselves the treasure of a good foundation for the future, so that they may take hold of that which is life indeed"—is the first hint in this passage that the use of our money has very real spiritual implications.

You may think that the way you use your money is a relatively little thing. However, the Bible tells us that the way we think about money, and the way we use it, reveals a great deal about the condition of your soul. Do you use the material things God has given you in a faithful and godly fashion? This is an important question.

Luke 16:10-13 (NASB) has some answers. Verse 10 explains the general truth that "He who is faithful in a very little thing is faithful also in much; and he who is unrighteous in a very little thing is unrighteous also in much." Rarely will you find an exception. Verse 11 continues, "Therefore if you have not been faithful in the use of unrighteous wealth, who will entrust the true riches to you?" True riches are spiritual riches. I speak of growth in grace and knowledge of God's Word. I speak of the great treasure that is peace. What greater treasure can we own on this earth than peace of conscience toward God? If you do not deal faithfully and righteously with temporary treasure—money—it is highly likely that you are still a captive of your own lusts and no servant of God. That being the case, you will not come to possess real and eternal treasure.

That leads to verse 12, which asks, "And if you have not been faithful in the use of that which is another's, who will give you that which is your own?" The steward was not faithful in managing his master's money. Therefore, he was fired and had nothing of his own.

As believers, our Master is God, and everything we have is His. We are only managers of our lives, talents, children, stuff, and, in this case, money. What can we call our own? Only the gifts of salvation, peace, contentment, maturity, and wisdom are given to the faithful steward. They are entrusted to the man who has been given a new heart. This man no longer serves his flesh but serves God and his fellow man.

Finally, verse 13 finishes the parable by stating, "No servant can serve two masters; for either he will hate the one and love the other, or else he will be devoted to one and despise the other. You cannot serve God and wealth." The Pharisees could not serve God because they were servants of themselves. The steward could not serve his master because of his love for money. We cannot serve God and anything or anyone else. There is no room for compromise here.

To be a child of God and a good manager of our lives and possessions, we must be totally devoted to Him by faith in Jesus Christ. We must be given over to using all we are and all we have to the glory of God. In this way, we will do ourselves the most good. In this way, we will lay up for ourselves treasures in heaven which will be ours alone, and which moth and rust cannot destroy.

FAITHFUL STEWARDS ARE BLESSED

In Matthew 25:14-46, Jesus explains to us how He will bless His trustworthy stewards. Their faithfulness in financial matters will cause Him to increase their belongings. He says the Kingdom of God is as a man who is going to travel into a far country who first calls his own servants (stewards) to him. He doesn't call someone else's servants— he calls his own.

Then, Jesus says this man delivers to these stewards various amounts of his money (a talent is a measure of money). He gives one five talents; another, two; and the third, one. Notice that the master gives money to his stewards, to redistribute as he directs them.

In the parable, the steward with five talents goes about his master's business and gains five more talents. Verses 19-21 tell us that, when he reckons with him, the master generously rewards his steward for his faithfulness. He essentially says to him, "Well done, good and faithful servant. You have faithfully kept your focus on my business. Because you have diligently promoted and expanded that which is mine, I am now going to expand that which is yours by making you ruler over many things."

Faithful stewards who constantly focus their attention on funding the end-time harvest will come into superabundance. This plan of seedtime and harvest will not let you down if you don't let it down. From personal experience, I can bear witness to the fact that great abundance comes to those who constantly give into the gospel of Jesus Christ.

THE SOCIALLY-CORRECT MISTAKE

One more disturbing trend exists among many who attempt to prosper by biblical principles. It is a subtle thing that happens almost without notice.

Because of the evangelical emphasis of most faith churches, many of their converts come from lower socioeconomic levels of society. As these people begin to prosper, they are cast in with a part of society that is unfamiliar to them. As they progress up the corporate ladder, they begin to associate with the crowd the world calls "the right people." These "movers and shakers" want to be with people who can make things happen for them. They are conscious of projecting the right image.

All too often, when these individuals—good, common, down-to-earth people—move into higher social circles, they begin to feel that the wrong social crowd attends their church. They feel pressure to get into a church where the right people—people who can help them the most in their careers—go.

Whatever you do, when you start on the road of biblical economics, keep your money involved in a live church dedicated to evangelism. Be vigilant, and see to it that tithing and giving offerings to God are the main uses of your money. Always keep in mind that you are a steward of God; and as a steward, God requires you to be faithful.

MANIFESTING ABUNDANCE

I hope you can now see that Mark 4 is not the chopped up, disjointed array of unrelated thoughts that tradition portrays. Instead, it's a single revelation that continues, uninterrupted, for 41 verses. It is our Lord's magnificent teaching on the process of manifesting abundance.

It begins with the bold statement that Jesus is going to declare His doctrine. This chapter illustrates a sower planting his seed. The full spiritual meaning of the chapter is that God gives potential for harvest-proportion increase to anything He calls "a seed." Our Lord then teaches that all truth is parallel. Whatever is true in the natural world is also true in the spiritual world. He shows us that parables are nothing more than parallels.

Verse 21 seems to be a transition, switching the subject to candles, bushels, and beds. However, it actually turns out to be the criterion for participating in the exceeding abundance that is above all we can ask or think, talked about in Ephesians 3:20. Yes, you must place your spirit-man on the candlestick. Your spirit must rule, or God will not make the secrets of Kingdom increase known to you.

Then, Mark reveals that we must understand God's principles of increase before we can take over the wealth of the world as described in Proverbs 13:22. Warning lights go on, and we find that God's way to abundance is not a get-rich-quick scheme. In God's way, growth comes slowly. It comes first as a blade, then a stalk, then the harvest. Warning lights should come on again as Jesus instructs us to keep our focus ever upward. If we take our eyes off Kingdom principles, we soon lose God's power to "make wealth," according to Deuteronomy 8:18.

Finally comes the clear teaching of the pastor and the church in the matter of the storm. It's impossible to maximize harvest increase without the guidance of a true pastor. When you put all these lessons together with other concepts our Lord will reveal to you from Mark 4, life will begin to progress, as the prophet said it would. You will have a firm hold on what Jesus taught about manifesting abundance, and victories will begin to multiply.

Brandon Mueller personally testifies to God's blessing in his life, proving God's faithfulness to good stewards:

> As I look back over the past few years, I really am in awe of how faithful God is. I have had the privilege of good mentoring through my parents and Pastor Chris, and I learned very early about making wise choices and investments.
>
> The first thing that is ultimately important in stewardship is keeping God first by paying your tithes. I feel that I have been blessed not because I am so good, but because God honors His Word. I have always been faithful with my tithe and offering, and that is the beginning of stewardship. God will surely open up the windows of heaven and pour out more than you have room to receive. I feel rather guilty saying "I" because, in all actual fact, I don't feel worthy to say that "I" have done anything so great as to deserve all that God has and is doing for me.
>
> I know that I am highly favored; but at the same time, there are principles that work for you, if you apply them. It's no secret that, if you are faithful over a little, God will make you ruler over much. Whatever it is God has blessed me with, I have taken care of it and not thrown caution to the wind.
>
> It's vital that, after you pay your tithe and offering, you make wise financial choices and investments that will not only sustain you but that will also be a cushion for you in "hard times." Everyone has hard times, but when you make wise financial choices and don't live beyond your means, it makes for a smoother transition.
>
> Another thing that is important is setting reasonable goals. You should also surround yourself with those who are striving to go where you are headed, and take care of what God has blessed you with. When God sees that He can trust you, He will open doors of opportunity for you and give you favor that is unimaginable. I know God will do it if you honor Him, and take care of what He has blessed you with.

I am only 24, but I have been blessed— not only to have my own home, but to have made investments that allow me to be a landlord, own my cars, and live a very rewarding life. It's not a fairy tale, and God's Word doesn't lie. Where much is given, much is required. The questions now are, "How much do you want?" and "How much are you willing to sacrifice in order to be ruler over many?" Being a good steward calls for discipline, but once you have put it into practice, it is very rewarding.

A VIEW FROM THE PEW

Four Stewardship Views Contrasted

America's churches and Christians' minds are flooded with imbalanced stewardship views. This chart contrasts three erroneous theologies to a balanced biblical theology of stewardship matters.

	Poverty Theology	Prosperity Theology	The American Dream Theology	Balanced Biblical Stewardship Theology
View of Prosperity	Prosperity is immoral. Possessions are disdained.	Prosperity is the reward of the righteous.	The pursuit of household possessions and family pleasures is acceptable.	Possessions are a trust given by God in varying proportions.
In a word, possessions are...	A curse	A reward	A right	A privilege
View about purchases	Least expensive and lowest quality	Top quality	Quantity	Wisest
"Proof text" Scriptural references	Sell all and give to the poor. (Luke 18:18-22)	Ask, seek, knock, and it shall be given to you. (Matthew 7:7-8)	You're worse than an infidel if you don't care for your own family. (1 Timothy 5:8; Haggai 1, where God's people were busy with their own households)	Parable of the Talents (Matthew 25:14-30)
Needs are met by...	Thinking you don't have any needs	"Seed faith" and "give to get"	Credit and borrowing	Faithfully using and giving what you've received
Primary Role	Rejecter	Owner	Accumulator	Steward (Manager)
Preoccupation	Daily sustenance	Money	Comfort and convenience	Wisdom
Attitude	Carefree (Proverbs 3:5-6)	Driven (Proverbs 10:17)	Entangled (Mark 4:19; Hag. 1)	Faithful (Luke 16:10-11)

If you are presently NOT faithfully giving to the Lord at least 10 percent of your income, I encourage you to read Haggai 1:4-11 and Malachi 3:8-10. Then, immediately begin to give to God at least 10 percent for the next 30-90 days. See if the Lord will not work in your life in creative ways. You'll never regret this decision!

As Christ relates to us the Parable of the Unjust Steward, we must not forget what had happened before. In chapter 15, He rebuked the Pharisees for their lack of love for the lost. By using the three parables in chapter 16, He illustrated the love of God for sinners and spoke of joy in heaven when even one sinner repents.

Biblical stewardship recognizes God as the ultimate source of all things. 2 Corinthians 9:8 states, "And God is able to bless you abundantly, so that in all things at all times, having all that you need, you will abound in every good work."

OBEDIENT STEWARDSHIP GROWS THROUGH TRUSTING GOD

I Kings 17:14-15 describes how God provided for Elijah and the widow at Zarephath. "For this is what the Lord, the God of Israel, says: 'The jar of flour will not be used up and the jug of oil will not run dry until the day the Lord gives rain on the land.' She went away and did as Elijah had told her. So there was food every day for Elijah and for the woman and her family."

Two great things happened. First, Elijah obeyed. Then, God supplied.

OBEDIENT STEWARDSHIP INVOLVES SEVERAL SMALL STEPS

Baby Steps for the New Giver:

- Give God the first portion—Proverbs 3:9
- Give regularly—I Corinthians 16:2
- Give God a percentage—Leviticus 27:30
- Give thankfully—Ephesians 5:20
- Give *something*!

* ★ ★ ★ ★ ★

STEP #5—ADMITTING YOUR NEED FOR A BUDGET

BUDGETING IS NOT A CURSE WORD! AS we move into this chapter, you must start monitoring your expenses in order to get your family on the path to financial health.

If you're asking why you need a budget, simply answer this question: "Do you know where your paycheck goes?" If not, it's time to start budgeting. You need to begin keeping track of your own expenses. Then, if that isn't daunting enough, you need to move on to monitoring the spending of your entire family. That takes even more effort and commitment! If you start small and involve everyone in the process, you'll be on your way to a working family budget and a plan for your financial future.

Neomia Coleman realized she needed a budget:

> After experiencing, to a certain degree, the benefits of living debt-free, we found ourselves launched into a different realm of experience with God in our finances. After quitting our jobs and moving to Atlanta in 2001, we found ourselves

in need of finances due to ten months of no income. Up to this time, we had lived off our savings and financial seeds that had been sown into our lives by others.

We'd learned about budgeting and benefited from it; but now, the question was this: "How do you budget with no income?" We weren't making any money, but we still needed to see where our money was going. We still had bills. Bills do not stop coming just because your incomes stops. We found ourselves in a quandary.

Budgets serve as guidelines for your finances. It does not matter if you have income or not—you still have to live somewhere, eat food, purchase gas, and pay utilities. It costs to live. The Bible says that you must count the cost before you spend. Setting up a budget will help you to count the cost. We will admit, it was hard to set up a budget in our situation. However, having a budget in place made us more responsible to our financial obligations, and it helped us know just how much income it took to run our household.

We kept a log of everything we spent for a month. This served a two-fold purpose. We moved from the Midwest,where cost of housing is much cheaper. We were experiencing a new area where things were different, so we compared prices on just about everything. Inasmuch as this was exciting, the bills kept rolling in while the income did not. We resorted to using our credit card, which had a zero balance (we had previously learned that the correct way to use a credit card was to pay off the balance each month when the bill was due).

Quickly, we racked up $5,000 on the credit card just with day-to-day living. It was painful, as it seemed that we were going backward instead of moving forward. One thing about bills and bill collectors is that they don't care about the circumstances that got you into the predicament; they just want to be paid! We paid our rent, utilities, and food for about three months using a credit card, and managed to make the minimum payment each month. It was hard, but it helped us set up our new budget.

Our son was two years old, so we were faced with another problem: Even if I found a job, who would keep our child? We were new to the city and knew no one. My husband finally landed a job. The only problem was it did not pay nearly the amount it would take to cover our basic budget. Then, we faced another challenge in our new life: I found that I was pregnant, which further restrained me from working. It's during the tough times, though, that having a budget in place—whether you can meet it or not—is very important. Sometimes, it simply serves to inform you of how much you are spending month to month.

Having a budget in place sets you up to be blessed. God can truly bless you to become debt-free if you know how much you are in debt. It's necessary to have a budget because, if you encounter a financial blessing—whether it is $50 or $500—you will know exactly where you need to apply it. God never allows us to hide from troubles; He expects us to face them and present them to Him. Having a budget in place opens the windows of heaven for you.

To make matters worse, after my husband got a job, we started to have serious car troubles and then had to move due to circumstances beyond or control. I was pregnant, we had a young child, my husband needed transportation for work, and we had to move. What a challenge! We found a place to live, but our car problems worsened. What do you do? We didn't have enough income to support the family—how would we afford a car? Because we had a budget in place, we knew that we had no money to buy a new car, nor could we afford one. But God was faithful in that we were able to purchase a vehicle that allowed us to pay what our budget could afford month-to-month with no interest.

Because we never stopped giving to the Lord and we had a budget in place, people were willing to sow financially in our lives. When we were asked how much could we afford for a car payment, I could quickly answer because we had a budget in place. A budget also helps your vision. When you have a budget in place, you know how to pray and what to pray for. Plus, you never know who has your blessings, and numbers don't lie. So if you have a budget in place, you can quickly give an answer—as the Bible instructs us—to anyone willing to help. Remember, prayer changes people, and people change things. Keep praying.

Take budgeting baby steps and start by tracking your grocery and food budget for a month, including restaurant meals, coffee shop treats, and vending machine snacks. Keep all receipts and write down what you spent for an entire month. You'll be surprised to discover how quickly the restaurant visits, and cokes or cups of coffee add up. When the month is over, you' have already tracked a major category of your household budget—congratulations!

Now that you've seen the change in your spending in these areas, set up more categories. Some expenditures vary little from month to month: housing (mortgage or rent), utility bills, insurance, and day-care. Others can fluctuate: entertainment, travel, home improvement, and auto repair. Devise some basic categories, adding or combining categories after you have a few months of budgeting under your belt. Get your spouse involved in the process. If he or she doesn't want to take part in recording or analyzing, at least make sure you get receipts for any purchases that your partner makes.

You can also invest in a budget software program. Microsoft Money and Quicken are the big names in personal budgeting soft-ware. Both are easy to use and generate numerous useful reports and forecasts. These programs help you organize your budget and make tasks like tax preparation a breeze.

Make sure you include the children. Give a small portion of your budget to your kids to control, and they'll learn the basics of earning and spending wisely while they're young. The snack food or dining-out portion of your budget is a good place to start with your pint-sized financial planner. When your kid sees how much two pizzas, four sodas, and a round of ice cream sundaes takes out of the monthly allotment, he may even stop begging to eat out every Friday night.

One of the things I learned very quickly raising three boys was that, when we go on vacation, I give them an allotted amount of money for the week. They can do with it whatever they choose. They can spend it all at once, they can buy extra soda away from the meals that we provide, or they can go on a shopping spree. It's totally up to them. However, they know that, when it is gone, there is no more. If they think you are paying for everything, they will take you for a ride—a very long one. But when they have to manage their money and make it last, only one time on the go carts is enough, compared to when Dad was paying and I would hear over and over, "Can we go just one more time?"

You must analyze, cut unnecessary spending, and start saving! Look at your spending habits with a critical eye and cut where you can if you have debt or if you're not putting enough away for savings. Better yet, include a monthly savings goal in your budget and have that amount automatically withdrawn from your paycheck and deposited into an account. The Bible says in Proverbs 21:20, "The wise store up choice food and olive oil, but fools gulp theirs down."

Make your budget easy enough that you'll keep at it. Don't get too fancy with your categories. The hassle of deciding where a particular expenditure fits may prevent you from continuing with your record-keeping. Find a central place for receipts and pick a time to do your paperwork. Once or twice a week is fine.

I hope you see the need for a budget in your life. I use an old saying from time to time with my congregation: "You are going to keep getting what you are getting, as long as you keep giving what you are giving." Just by picking this book up, you are showing that you're ready to make some changes in your life. Make them, so that your windows will be swung open and God can rain your blessing in through them.

* * * * *

STEP #6—ALLOTTING ROOM FOR MONUMENT OFFERINGS

I NEVER WILL FORGET THE DAY I TRULY understood "Monument Offerings." It was a cold night in the winter of 1987. My wife and I lived in a single-wide trailer we could not afford. I'd just started a new job as a youth pastor making $50 per week, and needless to say, ends were just not being met. We went to a church meeting where the pastor was talking about growth. The church was trying to buy a house next to it for further expansion. I remember, as he was talking, there was something inside of me seeing the vision and leaping. After a few moments, I jumped up and said, "I want to be the first to donate!"

It would have been all right if I stopped there, but I went on to say, "I will give $1,000 in 30 days." As I sat down, I could not believe what I'd just done. My wife was sitting beside me looking as if I had totally lost my mind. I didn't mean to do it. I didn't even think about doing it; it just happened. We were already talking about filing for bankruptcy, and we had literally $1.98 in the checking account. As

I sat back down in the pew, I began to get sick. I don't believe in making a vow and not keeping it; and even if we gave our entire checks from then until the 30 days were up, it would not come close to the $1,000 I had just pledged. I don't remember another thing that was said for the rest of the meeting. I was in total shock at what had just overtaken and spoken through me. Trust me, I didn't have that much faith.

After the meeting was adjourned, a gentleman came to me and handed me a phone number and said someone had called during the meeting and needed to speak to me desperately. As I drove home in quietness, my mind was going in a thousand directions—literally. When I arrived home, I called the number and the gentleman on the other end of the line said, "So, I hear you may be interested in selling your mobile home." I had no idea how he knew that, but the next morning, I met with him and we agreed on a price.

After paying our debts, we had $1,250 left over. You guessed it: the first $1,000 went to my pledge, and we did not have to file for bankruptcy. It all happened in less than 12 hours from the time we made the monument offering. God started turning our lives around at that very moment. I'm a firm believer that, as you make a monument offering, God will honor it, open up the floodgates of heaven, and pour out a blessing.

As you read this chapter, there are some very important things you must understand about such an offering. Pay close attention in your reading to how it works if you want a monument offering to move the hand of God in your finances.

WHAT IS A MONUMENT OFFERING?

A monument offering is an offering that you make...

- That is a sacrifice
- That has in mind a specific need to be met
- That you are determined to see come to pass

HOW DO I MAKE A MONUMENT OFFERING?

- Select a worthy recipient or cause, so that you sow into good soil.
- Choose an amount that HURTS when you give it.
- Let it represent something so BIG that you cannot do it yourself.
- Determine if it's a one-time offering or a set amount over a set period of time.

WHAT ARE SOME EXAMPLES OF MONUMENT OFFERINGS?

- One month's salary
- Your income tax return
- A percentage of your income
- Any large amount that would be a sacrifice

SPECIFICALLY, WHY SHOULD I MAKE A MONUMENT OFFERING?

- To become debt-free
- To break generational curses off your finances
- To break the mentality that you will always owe somebody something
- To get promotions and raises
- To become a lender and not a borrower
- To own your own business, etc.

★ ★ ★ ★ ★

STEP #7—ACHIEVING THE PRINCIPLE OF SOWING

BRENDA CHAND HAD A HEART FOR GIVING to God at an early age. Be blessed as you read her personal story of how she has reaped the benefits of sowing into God's work:

I can trace my love for giving back at least 47 years, to when I was seven years old. One day, I found a coin while playing outside. Even though, in those days, it could be used to buy candy (a rare treat), I desired to give it to God instead. Being only slightly churched, I didn't know the proper channels for giving an offering to God. I hurled the coin into a field expecting that He would receive it. I believe He did, and I think He decided to trust me with more and more resources as the years went on.

As a young child, I was a daydreamer. Even though I grew up in extreme poverty—at times, the seven of us in my immediate family lived in one room—I dreamed of one day having money and giving it to people in need. In my dreams,

I had this never-ending source of money, and I surprised my family by giving them unexpected money to meet their needs.

My history of giving has not always been perfect. At the age of eighteen, after several childhood experiences with God, I became a Christian. Soon after, I understood and attempted to practice tithing and giving. While attending Beulah Heights Bible College, after paying my bills—including tithes—I would have $20.00 per month left for my personal needs. There were times I would fall behind on giving and catch up by giving almost every bit of the personal resources I had at a later time.

The practice of tithing followed me into my marriage. My husband was also a tithe payer and giver. In the early years of our marriage, we challenged other couples to practice tithing. We made offers of paying their bills for them if they tithed and came up short. After a few years of marriage and tithe paying, that discipline was set in stone. Tithing came first, before other bills were paid. There was always enough money to meet our needs, and we loved the joy of giving to others.

Again, the history behind coming to that point is not perfect. There were a couple of times we got into credit card debt and had to take drastic measures to get out. The first time it happened, we had to consolidate, which resulted in having one large monthly payment that took two years to pay off. It was so high, and it required us to be so disciplined in our personal spending, that we were unable to make any purchases apart from necessities. And, believe it or not, we let the same thing happen a second time. We determined at that point that it would not happen again, and it hasn't.

A real breakthrough in giving came for me over ten years ago. One Sunday in church, there was an appeal for at least five people to give $1,000 to our pastor in appreciation. One of my primary gifts is giving, and when I hear of a need or someone makes such an appeal, my nature is to respond by giving. I raised my hand in pledge to give. When I told my husband, his response was favorable, but he wanted us to pay it in $250 increments so that it would not be a hardship.

On the exact day of the first $250 installment, someone told my husband they were going to start giving us $1,000 per month just to enhance our personal income. They followed up by giving us $1,000 each month for the next year. This person increased it to $2,000 per month for the following year, and it has continued to increase even now. That single incident let me know beyond any doubt that God is the source of my resources. It gave me the faith to believe God for any amount of money that is needed for myself, others, or organizations in need.

Today, my husband and I continue to give the maximum we can. Our written financial core values include: tithing on all gross income; determining how much is enough to live on, save, and invest; and giving the rest away to minister to people. We have set a goal for the amount of money we need for retirement. One of our long-term goals is to practice reverse tithing—we want to give 90 percent of our income and live on 10 percent.

I have fulfilled my childhood dreams of giving to my immediate family. At Christmas time—as well as in other times of need—I am able to give each family member a significant amount of money. We have invested in a home in a prestigious neighborhood. Through the help of our many friends, we are building a Bible college in India in memory of my father-in-law, who pastored and planted churches in India for over 49 years.

My financial story can be summed up by saying, "Little becomes much when you place it in the Master's hand."

SEEDS, BUSHELS, BEDS, AND A STORM

Jesus told and retold the story of the sower in the form of a parable. Then, there is a verse about a candle, a bushel, and a bed. This verse alerted me to the fact that I should be careful with an agricultural crop and the need for its timely harvest. It told me that a mustard seed could potentially grow into a very large tree. It could grow so big that birds could rest in its branches. The chapter ends with the story about a storm at sea and how Jesus stopped it. The fourth chapter of Mark is most surely the doctrine of Jesus Christ. In it, He keeps His promise to open the parables to us. The best part is that He shows us how to manifest abundance according to the principles of biblical economics.

Let me give a short overview. When Mark opens the chapter, Jesus is speaking to a multitude at the seaside. I have already alerted you to the major significance of verse 2, since Jesus is about to give us His doctrine. He will be revealing a part of the mind of Christ.

In verses 3-8, Jesus speaks of the Parable of the Sower. The Parable of the Sower is probably our Lord's best-known discourse. He tells of four terrains on which the sower places his seed. Three of these produce little or no harvest. However, one brings forth 30-, 60-, and even a 100-fold harvest.

Jesus closes this portion of the teaching in verse 9 by instructing His hearers to hear what He says. It is obvious from the context that He wants them to do more than just hear the sound of His voice—He wants them to understand fully what He is saying.

In verses 10-12, Jesus identifies the ones who will be able to bring forth abundance: it will be those who understand. In verse 13, He reveals the key to all the parables—He says those who understand this one will be able to understand all of them.

Notice in verses 14-20, when He repeats the parable, that Jesus makes a small but significant change: the seed He now speaks of is no longer an agricultural seed. It is the Word of God. Notice that this "seed" responds exactly the same way the agricultural seed does.

God gives the power to reproduce to any concept He calls a seed. Verse 21 is the verse that tends to block the flow of the whole chapter. Traditional explanations do little to help, as the subject abruptly changes from sowing and reaping to beds, bushels, and candles. When you see what Jesus is actually saying in this verse, the roadblock immediately comes down, and all 41 verses flow into one uninterrupted revelation.

God wants to talk to you about the secrets of manifesting abundance. Pay attention, for you will not understand verses 24 and 25 until you fully understand verse 23.

When you understand the implied subject, a primary principle of biblical economics becomes yours. Understanding timing and seasons is necessary to manifest abundance. The manifestation of abundance comes only to those who strictly obey God's Kingdom principles in the distribution of their harvest.

Starting in verse 35, there is a shift, and the apostle Mark now does the teaching. He points out the essential part a competent pastor plays in the manifestation of abundance. The true pastor is not afraid to minister to the real problems of his sheep. He also never abandons the message of faith.

I realize this overview has been sketchy, to say the least. However, I do hope it has shown you that these 41 verses hold a greater truth than the mixed teaching of traditional commentators reveals. These verses contain one continual, unbroken teaching that instructs the believer in our Lord's doctrine of manifesting abundance. Let's now proceed with an expanded teaching of these marvelous verses.

Sowing usually refers to planting agricultural seed. People throughout the world know the parable of the farmer who sowed his seed. Jesus gives us four circumstances that might take place when the farmer plants agricultural seed.

First, the seed can fall by the wayside and become food for the birds (verse 4). These seeds bring no harvest for man.

Next, Jesus tells of seed that falls onto stony ground. It brings forth a sprout. However, the shallow ground is unable to sustain normal growth. Where there is no depth of soil, a proper root system cannot develop. This lack of soil causes the plant to wither long before it can bring forth any kind of fruit (verses 5 and 6).

Then, Jesus tells about seed the farmer sows among thorns (verse 7). How foolish it seems to sow seed in a thorn patch. However, if you compare this account with the one in the book of Luke, you see that thorn-infested soil can sometimes appear to be good ground. In Luke 8:7, the writer tells us that the ground already contained the seed of weeds. Upon closer observation, you'll find that weeds don't actually appear until a crop begins to grow. After three failed attempts, the sower finally gets it right: he sows into good ground and receives the miracle of harvest-proportion returns.

After He gave this purely agricultural illustration, Jesus' disciples pondered the meaning of the story. Verse 10 tells us that, as soon as they were alone, they asked the Lord to explain the parable. Knowing our Lord as they did, they were sure the parable contained more than just agricultural information. At this point, Jesus relates to them the importance of spiritual understanding. He tells them that He uses parables to keep the mysteries of the Kingdom of God from those who are not of the Kingdom (verses 11 and 12.) Then, He makes a powerful statement: He says that the person who is able to understand this parable can understand all the parables.

The key our Lord was giving His disciples is that all truth is parallel. Whatever is true in the natural realm will also be true in the spiritual. Always look for the basic truth in the natural illustration, and you will find that same truth in its spiritual counterpart. Remember, parables are nothing more than parallels. Notice that, when Jesus restates the parable, the seed He speaks of in verse 14 is very different from the seed He uses in verse 3. Jesus has replaced the agricultural seed with the Word. Obviously, the Word of God is not an agricultural seed. Words and seeds are different.

Here's another difference between the two versions of the parable: in the spiritual application, the sower doesn't plant the Word in the field; he sows it into the hearts of men. However, Jesus says the results of preaching the Word of God are parallel to the results of planting agricultural seed.

Now, notice other parallels between the two stories: When the sower plants the Word of God into hearts that are like the wayside, Satan steals it (verse 15). When he sows into stony hearts, no root system develops. At the first sign of persecution, the new convert gives up (verses 16 and 17). When the sower plants the Word in a weed-infested heart, double-mindedness eventually causes the Word to lose its ability to bear fruit (verses 18 and 19). However, when he sows the Word into hearts having good ground, harvest-proportion increases take place bringing forth 30-, 60-, and even 100-fold harvests (verse 20). When a Christian sows the Word, the same results take place as when a farmer sows the agricultural seed.

Let me be clear about this one thing: God is the only one who can give reproductive power. Evolution didn't give seed the power to reproduce; neither did the fictitious being called "Mother Nature." God gives the power to reproduce to everything He calls a "seed." With the power to reproduce also comes the potential for abundant returns. However, harvest can happen only if you plant your seed in good ground. Scripture tells us God has assigned seed-power to a number of things. In the next chapter, we are going to take a moment to look at just a few assigned seeds—powers that God has given us to use in our lives.

Look at how perfectly this fresh revelation fits with the things the Holy Spirit has been revealing to the Body of Christ during the last few years. We have only recently begun to understand that money we give into the gospel is seed. However, we have hindered its potential by yoking it with the snail's-pace increase of Luke 6:38. Without realizing it, we have yoked the ox with the ass (Deuteronomy 22:10). In making this statement, I don't intend dishonor to the truth of Luke 6:38. I am merely showing how incompatible the slow growth rate of Luke 6:38 is compared to the explosive potential existing in every seed. Just imagine how much closer the Church would be to its goal of evangelizing the world if we harnessed the truth of seed-faith giving with the high-powered potential of harvest.

Why not just step out on the water of faith and go boldly where precious few have gone before? I challenge you to press into the high ground that lies beyond the scant increase. Go all the way, where 30-fold, 60-fold, and 100-fold harvests are commonplace. Enter the land of superabundance.

PRINCIPLE AND PROPORTION

I am not suggesting you scrap Luke 6:38, for it plays an important part in every offering. It establishes the principle of increase: whatever you give, God will return to you increased. However, it does not begin to approach the full potential of return you can receive from your giving. The proportion of increase always depends upon the quality of the ground and the degree of human intervention. If you plant in good ground and properly apply the laws of the harvest, your rate of increase can quickly grow into harvest proportions.

The second thing Luke 6:38 establishes is that your measure of return will be directly in proportion with the measure of your giving. If you plant an acre of wheat, you will not reap hundreds of acres of wheat. You will reap only the wheat that your acre brings forth. Paul reaffirms this truth when telling us that the farmer who plants little will reap little, and if he plants much, he will reap much (2 Corinthians 9:6).

Scant giving will never produce mega-returns. If you give with a thimble, you will restrict God to giving back to you in thimblefuls. If you give with a teaspoon, you can receive only teaspoonfuls multiplied back to you. However, if you give by the truckload, God will give back to you in truckloads.

SOWING IS NATURAL, HARVEST IS SUPERNATURAL

Keep in mind that the sowing of seed is a natural process. However, the manifestation of increase from a seed is a spiritual process. Farmers are not all religious people. However, the Word of God declares that every time a farmer (saved or lost) has a harvest, two things take place. First, he sows a natural seed. Then, supernatural intervention has to take place.

This verse tells us a miracle happens every time reproduction takes place. Notice that the farmer plants the seed; however, the actual process causing the increase is beyond his ability to understand—it's supernatural! The Word of God says, "...he knoweth not how." God must activate the life-multiplying power in every seed if there is to be an increase. As smart as he considers himself, man still cannot manufacture a seed that will reproduce by itself. Only God gives life.

A THREE-PART BEING

1 Thessalonians 5:23 says that you are made up of spirit, soul, and body. These three parts of your being are constantly striving for leadership of your life. When the soulish portion of your being rules, your life becomes a process of manipulation that accomplishes only selfish goals. When your body rules, it will strive to accomplish only those things that please it. It is impossible, under the leadership of either the body or the soul, to live a Christ-centered life. The reason is that "God is spirit…" (John 4:24), and He chooses to communicate primarily with man's spirit. It is as the Psalmist says: "Deep calleth unto deep…" (Psalms 42:7, KJV).

The apostle John tells us that a person who wishes to communicate with God must do so through his spirit. For God to lead you into the understanding that brings forth abundance, you must be constantly communicating with Him. To communicate with God, your spirit must dominate your life. Elihu, Job's friend, made an interesting statement about this communication. He pointed out that the spirit in man receives revelation from God. Elihu is saying that the Spirit of God breathes understanding into the spirit of man. The reason this is true is that the spirit of man corresponds to the substance of God.

GOD WANTS TO TALK TO YOU

In Mark 4:21-22, Jesus tells of the need for the dominance of the spirit man (candle) and why He wants our spirits to dominate. Let me paraphrase these verses to clarify further what they are saying. The spirit of a man should not be hidden. It must be in the position of leadership over the man, because nothing is hidden that will not be manifest. Neither will anything be kept secret (Luke 8:17). So only the spiritually-attuned ear will receive the wise counsel of God in manifesting abundance.

The breakthrough truth in these two verses quickly comes forth when we fully understand the candle. Placing your spirit man in control opens wide the door to understanding the whole chapter. All 41 verses can now speak to us about the doctrine of Jesus, which is the miracle of seedtime and harvest.

UNDERSTANDING AND RECEIVING

The truth breaks through with a word we find in Mark 4:9 and 4:23. The King James Version interprets this word as "hear." The Greek dictionary proves that translation of the word to be incomplete. Let's see how these two verses use it. The original word is #191 in the Greek dictionary of *Strong's Concordance*—it is the word *akouo*. The English word that accurately describes the intended meaning of this word in these verses is "understand," meaning "to understand the thing you are hearing." In Matthew's account of the parable of the sower, the translators translate it as "understand."

Verse 23 says that the saint who understands what he hears will receive in harvest proportions. When you apply this interpretation to the word in Mark 4:23, you see that our Lord is going on with His instructions about receiving the 30-, 60-, and 100-fold increase. Notice how clear it becomes when you use the word "understand" where the translators use the weaker "hear."

UNDERSTANDING REGULATES RECEIVING

Now we can understand the intended meaning of verses 24 and 25. Our Lord warns us to be very careful with what we understand. The traditional interpretation of this verse has clouded the reason Jesus gave this warning. We have always compared the measure in verse 24 to the measure in Luke 6:38.

Jesus is not speaking of the measure of Luke 6:38 in Mark 4:24. Keep in mind that He has been talking about understanding; so when the Lord says. "...with what measure ye mete [or give]," He is not referring to the amount a person gives. The subject Jesus has been discussing establishes the measure of Mark 4:24. See a true revelation of verse 24 as I now show you the proper context.

Paraphrased, it would be as follows: "'If any man has ears to understand, let him understand.' He said again to them, 'Be careful what you understand, because with whatever measure of understanding you do your giving, whatever you give will be measured back to you. Unto you who properly understand shall more be given.'" Clearly, our Lord is telling us that, with this new insight, the more you understand about Him and His Word when you give, the greater your rate of return will be.

★ ★ ★ ★ ★

STEP #8—ALWAYS REALIZING THE POWER OF YOUR SEED

APRIL THOMAS HAS TRULY REALIZED THE POWER of the seed:

I have learned a valuable lesson in sowing seed and reaping a harvest. Not too long ago, I received a letter from the IRS stating that I owed $10,000 and some change. They wanted the money right away, and I didn't have it. So I prayed and sought God on what to do. I confessed God's Word, that I owe no man anything but to love him. Not long after praying and confessing the Word of the Lord, He led me to sow a seed and name it, "debt freedom." It wasn't a large seed; I just listened for God to speak to me and did as the Holy Spirit said. I obeyed Him, and a few months later, God manifested.

I received another letter from the IRS apologizing and this time accompanied by a $4,000 refund. God then spoke to me and let me know that was not my harvest. He instructed me to sow the $4,000. I now wait with great expectation of what will manifest as a result of continuing to sow.

Never underestimate the power of a seed sown in fertile ground.

Seed Power: A Parable on Stewardship in Matthew 25:14-30

A Parable of What the Kingdom of Heaven Will Be Like (vv. 14-18)

(v. 14) Again, it will be like (The Kingdom of Heaven is a Stewardship of Christ's Resources) a man going on a journey, (Christ returns to Heaven at His Ascension.) who called his servants (Every believer has a vocation from Christ.) and entrusted his property to them. (Every believer has gifts from the Holy Spirit to serve Christ.)

(v. 15) To one he gave five talents of money, (A talent was worth more than $1,000.) to another two talents, (Various gifts are given by the sovereignty of the Spirit.) and to another one talent, each according to his ability. (We have different gifts matched with our abilities.) Then he went on his journey.

(v. 16) The man who received the 5 talents went at once and put his money to work and gained 5 more.

(v. 17) So also, the one with the two talents gained two more. (Each made a 100 percent return.)

(v. 18) The man who had received the one talent went off, dug a hole in the ground and hid his master's money. (He made no effort to advance the master's possessions. He did not lose or harm them, but he did not advance them either.)

Settling Accounts in the Kingdom of Heaven (vv. 19-27) (There Will be an Evaluation-Judgment of Believers)

(v. 19) After a long time the master of those servants returned and settled accounts with them. (Christ's second advent is delayed in time.)

(v. 20) The man who had received the five talents brought the other five. "Master," he said, "you entrusted me with five talents. See, I have gained five more."

(v. 21) His master replied, "Well done, good and faithful servant! (He's commended for obedience—not just faith.) You have been faithful with a few things; I will put you in charge of many things. (Leadership) Come and share your master's happiness!" (The joys of heaven await.)

(v. 22) The man with the two talents also came, "Master," he said, "you entrusted me with two talents; see, I have gained two more."

(v. 23) His master replied, (He produced less in quantity, but the same in percentage, and thus he receives the same commendation.) "Well done, good and faithful servant! You have been faithful with a few things; I will put you in charge of many things. Come and share your master's happiness!"

(v. 24) Then the man who had received the one talent came. "Master," he said, "I knew that you are a hard man, (Note the paralysis due to a wrong view of the fear of God.) harvesting where you have not sown and gathering where you have not scattered seed.

(v. 25) So I was afraid and went out and hid your talent in the ground. See, here is what belongs to you." ("I did no harm" is an insufficient defense.)

(v. 26) His master replied, (Note the response to this "sin of omission.") "You wicked, lazy servant! So you knew that I harvest where I have not sown and gather where I have not scattered seed?

(v. 27) Well then, you should have put my money on deposit with the bankers, so that when I returned I would have received it back with interest." (Capitalism has a biblical basis.)

The Final Destinies of Those Who Have Experienced the Kingdom of Heaven (vv. 28-30)

(v. 28) "Take the talent from him and give it to the one who has the ten talents. (We receive grace upon grace.)

(v. 29) For everyone who has will be given more, and he will have an abundance. Whoever does not have, even what he has will be taken from him. (Without grace, strict justice follows.)

(v. 30) And throw that worthless servant outside, into the darkness, (The judgment of Hell is the final end of unbelief and disobedience.) where there will be weeping and gnashing of teeth." (This is the opposite of "the master's happiness.")

A FAITH SEED

Jesus gave harvest potential to faith when He called it a "seed." Faith inside a good-ground heart responds the same way the mustard seed does when a farmer sows it into good ground. It starts out small, but it steadily grows. The apostle Paul tells us faith has potential for great increase.

A KINGDOM SEED

Jesus tells us the Kingdom of God has seed-power. Think about it. The Kingdom of God, which began as a tiny mustard seed, has now grown literally to fill the whole earth (Daniel 2:35). Surely, we must classify that kind of increase as harvest proportion. God has given to His Kingdom the same power He has given to every agricultural seed. Both faith and the Kingdom now have the potential for mega-increase. Daniel tells of the expansive power of the Kingdom of God in Daniel 2:44.

CHRISTIAN SEEDS

The entire Christian family is the spiritual seed of Abraham. God's Word said Abraham's seed would reproduce in harvest proportions. God said it would one day be as numerous as the stars of the sky. The multiplication of the Church is proof that the seed of Abraham has come forth in harvest proportions.

JESUS IS A SEED

When the disciples came saying that certain Greeks desired to see Him, our Lord's response seemed strange—that is, unless you understand that He looked upon Himself as a seed. He understood Himself to be the beginning of a totally new species that would one day populate the entire earth. In John 12:20-24, Jesus gives a strange answer when Philip simply asks if some visitors from Greece might see Him. While their request has nothing to do with farming, our Lord gives them an agricultural answer: He says that, unless it falls into the earth, the seed abides alone.

JESUS WASN'T SHOWING HIMSELF

To this day, our Lord's answer remains a mystery to most folks, for they don't understand that it was impossible for anyone to see Jesus at that time. The only person He presented to the world was His Father. Keep in mind that, only two chapters later, Jesus tells Philip that seeing Him is seeing His Father.

Our Lord's strange answer becomes clear when you understand that, if they wanted to see Jesus, the Greeks would have to wait until the seed (Jesus) was planted into the earth. After His death, burial, and resurrection, Jesus would bring forth sons and daughters who would change from glory unto glory into His image (2 Corinthians 3:18). It would be the job of this new species (the born-again believers in Christ) to show Jesus to the world.

When He spoke of the kernel of wheat falling into the ground and dying, Jesus was speaking of Himself. He was simply saying, "When I die and rise from the grave, I will bring forth many sons and daughters. They will show Me (Jesus) to the world."

MONEY GIVEN INTO THE GOSPEL

I have shown you God's ability to assign reproductive power to the things He calls "seed" in order to lay the groundwork for what I am about to share with you. God has given seed-power to the money you give into the gospel. When you give your money into the gospel, God automatically gives it seed-power. If you use wisdom and plant it in good-ground ministries, your money-seed has the potential of bringing forth a money-harvest.

In the same way that the sower who sows agricultural seed has the right to look forward to a superabundant yield, the sower of spiritual seed has the right to look forward to a superabundant yield. The overwhelming truth of this parable is that God automatically gives reproductive power (harvest potential) to everything He calls a "seed."

This truth also pertains to your money. When you give your hard-earned money to the gospel, God looks at it as a money-seed. This gives it the potential for massive multiplication.

In the verses between the two versions of the Parable of the Sower, Jesus gives us some other important information. He tells us who actually makes the request for more information about the parable. The request comes from a previously obscure group of people. Tradition leads us to believe it was the twelve apostles who asked. However, the language of verse ten indicates something quite different. You will see there is more here than we've been taught.

The Classic Amplified Bible brings light to what Mark tells us in Mark 4:11: "And He said to them, to you has been entrusted the mystery of the kingdom of God [that is, the secret counsels of God which are hidden from the ungodly]; but for those outside [of our circle] everything becomes a parable." This interpretation tells us that Jesus was speaking of Himself and His disciples (the twelve apostles and the other followers) as being in a circle. They were set apart from others.

Jesus goes on to tell us there is also a group outside the circle. He refers to them as "them that are without." He says the mysteries of the Kingdom of God are exclusively for those with Him inside the circle. These mysteries are not public information, but private revelation. A group of people inside the circle with Jesus understands—which is a better translation of the word—the mysteries of the Kingdom of God.

★　★　★　★　★

STEP #9—ALLOWING YOUR HARVEST TO REAP YOUR BENEFITS

YOU MAY BE A SINGLE PARENT STRUGGLING to provide for your family on a very limited income, but be encouraged by the personal experience of Juanita Lever, a widow who successfully raised her daughter while keeping God first in her giving:

> My tithes have always been the priority in my finances since the day I was saved. I have never missed or delayed giving to God what was His. After my husband died unexpectedly, and my daughter and I were left with less coming in to pay the same bills, God never let me down in the finance department. When I wondered where the money was coming from to pay a bill, the Lord was working it out, and I found I didn't have to worry. I received increases in my salary soon

after my husband's death. I knew this was the Lord because, as a rule, we only received one raise per year.

Over the years, the Lord has truly blessed me beyond measure. This has been not only in money, but in my health, in my possessions lasting longer than the usual stated time, and the supply of our wants. From our vacations to Amy's mission trips, God has always provided for me. When I hear someone say, "I can't afford to pay tithes," I can truthfully smile and say, "I can't afford not to."

LOOKING BEYOND LUKE 6:38

Tradition has made Luke 6:38 the favorite Scripture at offering time. Please remember that tradition can make the Word of God of no effect (Mark 7:13). There is a major problem with using Luke 6:38 in connection with giving money into the gospel. This verse promises a very poor rate of increase. It doesn't even begin to reach harvest proportions. It promises only a pressed-down, running over bushelful in return for each bushel you give.

Granted, it will be more than you gave. Yet, it will be a far cry from 30-, 60-, and 100-fold. The literal interpretation of Luke 6:38 doesn't even touch the hem of the garment of what Jesus proposes in Mark 4! The more you think about it, the more obvious it will become. Luke 6:38 does not speak of harvest-proportion returns. No farmer would farm if he had to plant a bushel of corn to harvest one overflowing bushel of corn. It wouldn't be worth the effort for such a puny rate of return.

As strange as it may seem, harvest is not a natural event. Nowhere in nature does it occur without human intervention. Let me illustrate for you. A grove of one hundred oak trees will yield literally thousands of acorns each year, but it won't bring forth thousands of additional oak trees each year. However, if a farmer gathers up all the acorns and places them in potting soil, carefully watering and nurturing them, the grove will produce thousands of oak trees each year. You see, harvest is not a natural event. A human being has to take dominion over the natural rate of increase and force it into the wondrous dimensions we call "harvest."

HARVEST PROPORTIONS WOULD CHANGE EVERYTHING.

If God's children could learn how to operate in the harvest principles of Mark 4, everything would quickly change for the Church. We would easily fund world missions. No longer would it be necessary to mortgage the gospel to build desperately-needed church facilities. With a full explanation of how to manifest abundance, no Christian would ever have to say no to funding the end-time harvest.

All we needed was a step-by-step plan. Only a few more words, and the mega-return of Mark 4 would be ours. However, the chapter seemed to contain no practical, step-by-step instructions. Unless I was missing something, superabundant increase would have to go on existing only in parable form.

DIVINE REVELATION CHANGES THINGS

The candle spoken of in this verse is meant to have a figurative application. Jesus is using the candle to represent the spirit of man. To prove this point, he turns our attention to a verse in the book of Proverbs. When He speaks of placing the candle on the candle stand, Jesus is not beginning a new thought. Verse 21 is not the brick wall I had thought. It is one of the most important steps a person must take to manifest harvest-proportion returns. Mega-harvest will be available only to those who will let their spirit control their life!

REVELATION STIRS REVELATION

Thank God, Mark 4 is no longer a series of disjointed thoughts! It is a complete revelation of how the believer is to manifest harvest-size increase. We all know good ground is necessary for an abundant harvest in the natural realm, but good ground is also necessary in the spiritual realm. To receive harvest-size returns, you must live a spirit-ruled life. The spirit-dominated life turns the natural heart (soul) into good ground.

HUMAN SPIRIT, NOT THE HOLY SPIRIT

When He speaks of walking in the spirit in Mark 4 (putting the candle on the candlestick), our Lord is not instructing us to walk in the Holy Spirit. The biblical meaning of walking in the spirit is the process of conducting the affairs of your life under the direction and control of your own, reborn, reliable, human spirit. Jesus is saying that if you want mega-harvest, you must let your human spirit control your life. Spiritual harvest principles will not function in the life of a Christian whose soul or flesh dominates him. Harvest-proportion returns come only to Christians whose spirit-man rules.

IT'S A BIBLICAL CONCEPT

The concept that what you receive increases as your understanding increases is not new. Think for a moment, and you will realize that receiving according to your understanding pertains to all Scriptural truth.

Understanding applies to the baptism in the Holy Ghost and speaking with other tongues. If you understand that God no longer gives the gift of tongues, you will find it difficult to receive the baptism of the Holy Ghost and your prayer language.

Your understanding also applies to divine healing. As long as you limit your understanding and believe divine healing ended with the death of the twelve apostles, it will be extremely difficult for you to receive divine healing. Your lack of understanding God's ongoing plan of healing His children will limit your ability to receive.

On the other hand, you can increase your understanding through studying God's Word, and recognize that God is the same yesterday, today, and forever (Hebrews 13:8). This increase in your understanding will enable you to believe that, if He ever healed anyone, God is still healing people today. You can go even farther and increase your understanding to know that, when the Roman soldiers laid stripes on the back of Jesus, those stripes purchased healing for everyone. This simple growth in understanding will immediately allow you to receive healing. Not only that, but it will also qualify you to deliver God's healing power to others by the laying on of your own hands.

JOHN THE BELOVED TAUGHT IT

What you just learned about increased understanding also brings increased prosperity. To see this truth, you must look with me at the prayer of the Apostle John. Remember that your soul is your mind (intellect), will, and emotions. The word that best sums up these three parts of the soul is "understanding." The main point of the Apostle John's prayer is not that you prosper, but that you prosper *in direct proportion to* your increase of understanding about prosperity. Hear the condition He lays down for prospering and being in health.

DON'T GIVE UP

When the promises of God seem difficult to receive, it's not time to give up on them. It's time to turn to the Word of God and increase your understanding about the promise that is eluding you. Don't allow yourself to pass up even one promise from God. He wants you to have all of them. He makes this fact crystal clear by saying that He doesn't tease us by offering promises He won't deliver on.

When receiving becomes difficult, don't give up. Just remember the instructions our Lord gives in Mark 4:24, where He says that with the same measure of understanding with which you do your giving, He will give back to you. Not only that, but keep in mind what the Apostle John says in 3 John 2: his top prayer is that your prosperity and health will increase as your understanding increases.

* ★ ★ ★ ★ ★ *

STEP #10—ALWAYS EXPECTING YOUR MANIFESTED ABUNDANCE

WHAT JESUS TAUGHT ABOUT "MANIFESTING ABUN-
DANCE" COMES to us at a very exciting time in the
plan of God. Do you know what time it is? It is over-and-
above-all-we-can-ask-or-think time.

It is over-and-above time in the financial realm. The Church has
reached the time of superabundance. Those who will enter are those
who are willing to believe the Word of God concerning Biblical prosperity. If we are willing and obedient, we will eat the good of the
land, according to Isaiah 1:19.

In Mark 10:17-30, the rich young ruler is not willing and obedient. He trusts in his money to the extent that he cannot obey God's
call to him. After he goes away sad and depressed, Jesus says, "How
hard it is for those who trust in riches to enter into God's way of
doing and being right." The disciples are astonished and ask, "Who
then can be saved?"

Jesus answers, "With men this is impossible, but not with God... Truly I tell you...no one who has left home or brothers or sisters or mother or father or children or fields for me and the gospel 30 will fail to receive a hundred times as much in this present age: homes, brothers, sisters, mothers, children and fields—along with persecutions—and in the age to come eternal life."

I believe the 100-fold return spoken of in Mark 10:30 is that what we've given for the gospel is coming back to those of us who believe, between now and the time we leave this earth. I believe now is the appointed time for the wealth of the sinner to come into the hands of the just (Proverbs 13:22). God didn't make the wealth of the earth for the devil and his children. God created this earth for His family. It belongs to us!

TOO GOOD TO BE TRUE?

Imagine getting back $30 for giving $1, getting $6,000 for giving $100, or getting $100,000 or more for giving $1,000. This rate of return sounds impossible to most folks. Does it sound impossible to you? Well, it didn't seem the least bit impossible to Jesus. In fact, He actually taught these outrageous rates of increase.

The great truth I am speaking of comes from the fourth chapter of Mark. This chapter contains two key verses that should have immediately put us on notice as to their extreme importance. Even though these verses have been crying out to the Church for 2,000 years, no one seems to have paid any attention to them.

We find the first of these wondrous sayings in Mark 4:2. This verse says that Jesus is about to reveal His doctrine to us! I am convinced the main reason we have gone this long without emphasizing the significance of this statement is because it deals with doctrine. So much division has taken place over doctrine that most Christians subconsciously tend to avoid it.

WHAT DOCTRINE IS

Let's take a moment and define what doctrine is. Simply stated, it is what an individual or group of individuals understands about

Scripture. To know what Presbyterians understand about God's Word, you must study Presbyterian doctrine. To know what Episcopalians believe, you must study Episcopalian doctrine, and so forth throughout the denominations.

WHAT JESUS UNDERSTOOD

With this definition of doctrine, let me once again draw your attention to verse 2 of Mark 4. This portion of Scripture is of tremendous importance, because it alerts us that Jesus will be telling us about His doctrine. If I know anything about Bible study, I know that its primary purpose is to promote understanding of what Jesus (God) is teaching. We want to understand the mind of Christ. It's there in black and white in Philippians 2:5. Mark 4:2 says Jesus is about to reveal some of the things He understands.

THE KEY PARABLE

A second verse in this chapter should also have caught our attention. It deals with parables. Just think about it: here we have the key that qualifies us to understand all parables. How is it that a verse with such tremendous promise could go virtually unnoticed for so long?

Jesus tells us that entering into the circle with Him is the first step to manifesting abundance through Biblical principles. To enter our Lord's circle, you must depart from darkness and enter into the light. You must exit the realm of natural thinking and enter the realm of supernatural thinking. Because we are sinners, separated from God, we must come into fellowship with Him.

Salvation takes place by accepting Jesus as your Savior. There are no two ways about it. God does not give the knowledge (understanding) of the mysteries of His Kingdom to those outside His circle. This wealth-gaining information comes only to those who are, as the Amplified Bible Classic Edition puts it, "inside the circle." Only this group will be able to understand Kingdom principles of increase.

THE CHURCH

Our Lord speaks of a relationship between a group of people assembled with a leader. The advanced students (the twelve), or better said, the sub-leaders of the group, surrounded the leader (Jesus.) Another group, consisting of less-advanced students and relatively new followers, surrounded those twelve (this example is a good picture of the local church). I cannot overemphasize this truth. The first steps in manifesting abundance by Kingdom principles are new birth and membership in a proper New Testament church. Just being born again isn't enough. You must also be part of a church that will nurture and help you grow up in Christ.

Remember, this parable opens all parables to you. Now get this: Sowers are farmers, and farmers are nurturers. They nurture the tender sprouts carefully, taking care of them by feeding, watering, and protecting them until they come into full stature. In John 3:3, Jesus states that being born again allows you only to see the Kingdom of God. Something else must take place before you can enter and enjoy its benefits. When will the Church learn that the preaching of the gospel only saves souls? The teaching of the Word of God *establishes* souls, causing them to experience the bountiful, new life God has for them.

Here's the bottom line: even if it falls onto good ground, a seed cannot bring forth a harvest unless there is a farmer to nurture it into its full potential. Neither can Christians bring forth the abundance God has planned for them without tender nurturing from a faithful pastor in a good local church. There is a circle. It's called the "local church." Abundance by Kingdom principles comes only to those who grow to full stature by submitting to the environment and the discipline of a proper local church.

In Mark 4, Jesus clearly speaks of receiving in much greater proportions than just shaken down and running over. He speaks of 30 bushels for 1, and 60 bushels for 1, and even 100 or more bushels for 1. It's obvious that this kind of return would quickly lead to abundance.

WHAT YOU BELIEVE AND SAY

Scripture plainly teaches that you will have whatever you say and believe. Understanding this truth should make a big difference in the proportion of increase you receive from future offerings.

As long as you confess a Luke 6:38 increase over your offerings, you will receive the meager rate of increase of that verse. Don't misunderstand—you will see an increase, but it will be no more than "pressed down, and shaken together, and running over." However, if you will boldly begin to speak the 30-fold, 60-fold, and 100-fold return over your offerings, you will be one step closer to receiving harvest-proportion returns. If you speak and fully believe in your heart that what you say will come to pass, you will have whatever you say (Mark 11:23). To move forward into this breakthrough, you will have to go beyond tradition into the realm of "rightly dividing the word of truth."

WHAT DOES 100-FOLD MEAN?

For many years, ministry has focused on the 100-fold return. What does 100-fold really mean? Is it 100 times? Is it 100 percent? Is it double? What does it really mean? For a long time, the only answer I was given was, "I don't know exactly what it meant."

BEST POSSIBLE

Let's take a look at what He has shown us. It is easy to understand what 30-fold and 60-fold mean. 30-fold means 30 times, and 60-fold means 60 times. However, 100-fold is much different. Notice that, in telling the story of the sower, Jesus breaks the mathematical progression He uses after reaching 60-fold. He progresses by 30 at a time until He gets beyond 60-fold. Then, instead of adding another 30 to His count and coming to 90-fold, he jumps 40 and ends with 100-fold.

To understand what Jesus is doing, we must realize that 100 is a unique number. It is the only one that can represent an indefinite amount of numbers. It can also mean "complete" or "the best possible."

In the classroom, 100 represents the best possible score. If you were to take a test with 100 questions, the best possible score would be 100. If the test had 25 questions, the best possible grade would not be 25. It would still be 100. Let's go one step farther. If a test had 200 questions on it, the best possible grade would not be 200. It would still be 100.

MORE THAN 100 TIMES

When it is planted in good ground, a little apple seed increases far more than 100 times. One apple seed produces one apple tree. To determine the yield of the seed properly, you must count all the apple seeds the tree brings forth in its lifetime. It could be tens of thousands of seeds.

The average apple has about five seeds in it. We could safely conclude that, if 100-fold meant only 100 times, a 100-fold apple seed could bring forth only about 20 apples. The mathematics are as follows: 20 apples times 5 apple seeds in each apple equals 100 apple seeds. However, we know that an apple tree can live many years, and can produce thousands of apples. This would mean that, in the case of apple seeds, 100-fold could easily equal tens of thousands of seeds. This information tells us that a 100-fold return can mean much more than just 100 times.

LESS THAN 100 TIMES

If 100-fold had to mean exactly 100 times, a cattle rancher could never experience the 100-fold return from a cow. The average cow reproduces only 1 calf per year. To bring forth 100 calves would take 100 years. That's longer than a cow's natural lifespan. As I understand it, a good breeder cow will birth about 9 calves during her reproductive years. More than 9 is considered exceptional. The best possible yield from a cow would be 9-13 calves. Therefore, 100-fold in the livestock industry (considering just the animals) would mean much less than 100 times.

From these two illustrations, you can see that 100-fold can represent differing amounts of increase. God has shown me through these examples that 100-fold has to mean the best possible yield. I have learned never to judge God's performance in my harvest until I have checked how the heathen come out with theirs. My God is the God of 30-fold and 60-fold and, no matter what the circumstances, He always gives me the best possible return! He always makes it 100-fold!

LUKE'S ACCOUNT

When you read the Parable of the Sower in Luke 8, the true meaning of 100-fold becomes even clearer. Luke doesn't even mention 30-fold and 60-fold. When you compare Luke 8:8 with Mark 4:8, there is no question that they are describing the same event. Mark's account says 30-fold, 60-fold, and 100-fold. Luke's says only 100-fold. This shows that 100-fold can mean any amount of increase.

I hope you can see that, with a 100-fold return, it is possible for you to manifest the superabundance Jesus teaches in Mark 4. If you keep yourself in a position to receive the best God has, it won't take long for every promise of blessing and abundance in God's Word to become yours. It will be as that Scripture says.

THE CANDLE REPRESENTING THE SPIRIT OF MAN

To understand the revelation of Mark 4 properly, you must know exactly what Jesus meant in verse 21 when He spoke of the candle.

THE BRICK WALL

Not fully understanding this verse will block the flow of the whole fourth chapter for you. Remember that, in the traditional interpretation, the candle presents a new subject that ends the teaching about receiving 30-fold, 60-fold, and 100-fold. Why would Jesus bring us to the threshold of mega-harvest (verses 8 and 20), and then, without finishing the thought, stop and begin a new discourse about beds, bushels, and candlesticks?

THE PROCESS

Notice, again, that Jesus uses a parable to illustrate the time needed for manifesting abundance. It is evident from the verses in Mark 4:26-28 that Jesus is not speaking of the timing associated with the world's method of accumulating abundance. In the uncertain system of this world, everyone tries to make money as fast as they can. Words such as "windfalls," "rip-offs," and "killings" are common in the financial realm of darkness. However, we are in the world, but not of the world (John 17:16). Our Lord is not inviting us to participate in the flawed process of natural wealth accumulation. Instead, He is showing us His unfailing principles of supernatural wealth accumulation.

THE TIMING

Jesus is describing the time needed for manifesting harvest-proportion increases. Hear it again: you must not only sow your seed into the good ground of the gospel, but you must also allow time to pass. The farmer sleeps and rises a number of times before his seed progresses to the next stage. During this time, the sprouts appear, grow, and increase. It is a process—not an event. It takes time. Many nights and days pass as the seed develops.

THREE DEFINITE PERIODS

Three distinct time periods divide the process leading to harvest: Our Lord calls them "the blade," "the ear," and "the full corn in the ear." It is important to understand these three stages of growth, for they prepare you for the definite changes that must take place in the seed as it moves toward harvest. Without clear understanding, the first two stages could cause you to become discouraged, and you could miss the harvest. However, when you understand them, these stages assure you that the seed is properly progressing. Once again, it depends on your understanding.

THE BLADE

After the farmer sows it, his seed is completely out of his control. For a while, it seems as if nothing is going to happen. The field looks empty for many days. During this barren season, patience is necessary. For those who have patience, by and by, a change takes place. The blade breaks through the soil, and everything takes on a new perspective. The process is working, and harvest is coming. However, blade time can be detrimental to harvest, for it brings the temptation to end the whole process by consuming the sprouts.

THE SPIRITUAL REALM

In the spiritual application of blade time, this same danger exists. As soon as you experience the first increase from giving, you may be tempted to spend it all on your personal needs and desires.

No doubt the disciples faced this same kind of temptation during the miracle feedings our Lord performed. Just think of the temptation when they saw fish and loaves rapidly multiplying in their hands. How tempting it must have been to set aside a few choice fish and some nice, fresh loaves for their own personal use.

Thank God that they didn't give in to their base instincts, for when the fish and loaves stopped multiplying in their hands, our Lord had not forgotten them. There were 12 large basketfuls leftover (Mark 6:35-44). Their patience brought them more than they could have ever hidden away while distributing the loaves and fishes.

Here it is in a nutshell: when the first signs of financial increase appear, don't stop giving. Just keep on planting and replanting. Make sure each successive time of sowing contains a greater portion of each new harvest.

The blade stage is to be a time of hope—not a season of foolishly eating up the sprouts. Let each sprout grow into a full harvest. Remember, harvesting sprouts brings nothing more than a Luke 6:38 return. It will be only a little bit more than you planted. However, if your faith, hope, and patience can prevail, allowing your seed to reach its full potential, God's Word says that it can yield 30-fold, 60-fold, and even 100-fold.

STALK TIME

The King James Version translates our Lord's words as "then the ear" (Mark 4:28). I'd like to call it "stalk time." It is after the tender sprout becomes a rough, rigid stalk. This phase of development seems the longest to the farmer. Not only does it take a long time, but the crop starts looking as if it has died.

HARVEST TIME

How wonderful it is when the farmer thrusts in the sickle and takes the harvest! The exhilaration of reaping is so totally satisfying that the farmer sows again and again toward even bigger harvests. It is an experience beyond description. This glorious feeling is especially wonderful when it comes in the financial realm. You have unspeakable joy when the fear of insufficiency is gone from your life. You can give freely again and again, knowing your Father's Word is true, and it will never fail you.

You have great comfort when you know that shortage can no longer come near your dwelling. Your supply no longer depends on the flawed system of the world. It depends on the unfailing promise of God that says, "While the earth remaineth, seedtime and harvest... shall not cease" (Genesis 8:22).

NOT AN EVENT

Remember, the manifesting of superabundance in the economy of God is never an instantaneous event. It is a time-consuming process. However, rest assured that the manifestation of 30-, 60-, and even 100-fold will be worth the time it takes. When it comes to full maturity, your heaven-sent harvest will be as the Scripture says: "exceeding abundantly above all we can ask or think" (Ephesians 3:20, KJV).

TRUE CHRISTIANITY IS EXPENSIVE

When you properly operate it, your Christianity quickly becomes the most expensive lifestyle a human being can undertake. I say this because, in its purest form, the gospel instructs us to feed the hungry

(Matthew 25:35-45). Notice it doesn't talk about just a few hungry people, but all the hungry. Now that's expensive! The gospel also instructs us to clothe the naked. That doesn't mean just a few of the naked, but all of them. Once again, we are talking about big money.

To demonstrate true Christianity, we must literally go into all the world and preach the good news to every creature. Every creature means every last one of them (Mark 16:15). It doesn't take a genius to understand that feeding all the hungry, clothing all the naked, and evangelizing all the lost will be the most expensive venture we have ever undertaken.

DIVINE ENABLING

When He placed the tremendous responsibility of world evangelism upon His Church, the Lord made Himself responsible for supplying the resources it would need to accomplish the task. Hear the angel Gabriel as he reassures us of this fact. The Bible tells us God has already approved and set aside all the supply we need to fulfill godliness. Hear the apostle as he reaffirms the availability of this exceeding abundance. Thank God that the Church doesn't have to depend on the worldly methods of increasing wealth. God has chosen the unfailing principles of seedtime and harvest to provide the wealth we need to fulfill the Great Commission.

THE LORD OF THE HARVEST

Our Lord makes a very important statement when He says that the farmer does not know how the seed becomes a plant. He isn't saying the farmer has no knowledge of the processes that take place in transforming a seed into a plant. He is simply saying the farmer does not have the ability to duplicate the process.

If they had 10 billion dollars to spend, the professors of the most advanced agricultural university in the world could not design, engineer, or produce a seed that could bring forth a living plant. Man simply cannot make a seed. He can enhance it so that it produces more; he can genetically alter a seed, bringing forth a mutation;

however, he cannot start with raw materials and produce a seed from scratch, for a seed contains life, and only God can give life.

When you fully understand it, this truth will become perfectly reasonable to you: God should share in your harvests, for there is never a harvest unless God does His part. He gives the power of reproduction to the seeds you plant. Yes, the farmer must work hard if he expects an abundant harvest. He must also plant in good soil. However, unless God does His part, there will never—under any circumstances—be a harvest.

Scripture clearly teaches that man is to reward the ox for plowing and that the laborer is worthy of his hire (pay). Just as the farmer deserves his portion of the increase, God is entitled to His share of everything that increases upon the earth, for He is the main contributor in all increase. Thank God that we don't have to guess how much His efforts are worth! He has already established the value of His contribution to every increase. He says His part will be 10 percent (the tithe).

Scripture is clear that God believes 10 percent of all the increase of the earth is not a gift to Him. Neither is it a tax. Rather, it is His appointed portion for His part in bringing forth increase.

No matter what the endeavor, if there is increase, God has a part in it. Whether it be the woodsman who sells a tree he has cut down, or the security guard who draws wages for 40 hours of work, Jehovah God plays a part in every person's increase. The woodsman owes God the tithe because he sold God's trees. The security guard owes 10 percent of his wages because God allowed him the 40 hours he spent earning his wage.

When He said the farmer did not know how the seed grew into a plant, our Lord was actually stating that Jehovah God makes an invaluable contribution to everything that increases. Therefore, God must receive His tithe. There will be no manifestation of abundance by biblical principles unless you pay the tithe that keeps heaven open over your seed (finances).

GROWING UPWARD

The requirement Jesus speaks of next is single-mindedness. The person successful in harvest will keep his finances involved in the business of the Kingdom of God. Our Lord tells us the seed growing into harvest proportions must continually grow upward.

DISTRACTION BRINGS DISASTER

How often I have seen people in a desperate season of their lives call upon the mercy of God for help! I am primarily speaking of those who said they would either receive a financial miracle or perish. When people reach this point, their giving to God usually comes as a last resort, but they pledge and pay. Then, when the promised abundance starts coming, they foolishly turn their finances away from funding the gospel and begin, once again, looking to worldly schemes for their increase.

Others hear the pastor speak from the Word of God about giving and receiving. Out of simple obedience, they begin to follow his instructions. This leads them to experience God's promised increase. Everything goes well until their financial assets become substantial. Then, all of a sudden, they begin to feel that their wealth has become too great to trust the advice of a mere pastor. Now they need tax consultants and financial planners.

Step-by-step, they leave off tithing and giving until they do little more than tip God. How subtly the devil works when he redirects a person's financial affairs! If your finances ever lose their upward focus, they will also lose their divine empowerment.

Tax consultants and financial planners have their place in the lives of God's children. Nevertheless, before they can properly help you, these experts must understand that your source is the God of heaven. You must inform them it is absolutely necessary for you to have an open heaven, meaning that tithes and offerings are not optional in your portfolio. You must let them know that no investment can ever come before your tithe and generous offerings. Make it plain. Even if it means passing up the deal of the century, you will not go one week without tithing.

CAUGHT IN THE TRAP

So many times, I have seen the children of God drawn away from the manifestation of abundance because someone suddenly came up with a great deal. It always sounds so simple: all they have to do is give up tithing and offerings for six short months. I can still hear them saying, "Trust me, Pastor. When this deal comes through, I will single-handedly fund the vision for the whole church."

Remember, the financial plan that grows into full harvest proportions is one that continually grows upward. It never gets out of focus with God's purpose. Don't worry about missing out on the "good life." As long as you fulfill God's purpose in your giving, God will let loose abundance into your hands.

Now that you have the power to open your window to financial freedom, I trust that you will put these simple principles into action so that your financial window will be swung open—not only for you, but for your children and your children's children. Your journey to financial freedom may not come easy, but God will help you as you put your hand to the plow to reap the harvest of abundance in your life. Let's become debt-free in the Kingdom of God.